Practice Sessions

A guide to accompanying the learner driver

Published by BSM
in association with
Virgin Publishing

Published in the UK in 2001 by
The British School of Motoring Ltd
1 Forest Road
Feltham
Middlesex TW13 7RR

Text by the Product Development Team, British School of Motoring

Cover picture and cartoons by Marc Lacey
Other illustrations, design, typesetting and repro by Thalamus Publishing

ISBN 0-7535-0559-2

Printed and bound in Italy

Contents

Foreword

Every year nearly a million new learner drivers take to the road. Their aim, I am sure, is to gain a full driving licence. To achieve this aim and to ensure a lifetime of driving enjoyment, it is important to prepare correctly.

There is no substitute for practical experience and the best way to gain this is by taking lessons with a good professional driving instructor who uses the most up-to-date teaching techniques in a modern, dual-controlled car.

The *Road Safety Strategy Document*, published by the Department of Environment & Transport in March 2000, highlighted the need for a structured approach to learning to drive. Research indicates that practically every learner who attempts the Practical Driving Test has had some professional tuition — an average of 30–35 hours of lessons. However, the research also showed that between one-third and half take no additional practice and, as a consequence, on average a novice driver only covers about 650 miles in supervised driving before taking their test.

Because newly-qualified young drivers have a significantly higher rate of accidents in their first year on the road, it is important that they should gain as much experience as possible before taking the test. The aim should be to try to put 'old heads on young shoulders'.

Practice Sessions has been developed by BSM in order to bring together the important aspects of learning and to make sure that the learner not only passes the test but that their future years of driving are enjoyable and safe. The book is not a substitute for professional training but offers a template through which additional experience can be gained in a constructive way.

As a person starts learning to drive, their BSM instructor will be able to recommend particular aspects of this book to an experienced driver who may accompany the learner. The BSM Track Record will also be an invaluable source of information to document the progress being made.

Formal training with a professional BSM instructor and informal practice with a non-professional accompanying driver are quite different but complementary learning experiences. Learning to drive and passing the Practical Test depends on the aptitude of the individual learner together with the total amount of driving experience in both formal and informal structures.

There are no shortcuts to becoming a safe and competent motorist. Learners should not stint on training or experience opportunities, since their safety depends on commitment to the learning process.

Practice Sessions and its companion BSM books on both the Practical and Theory Tests give the learner the best opportunity to become a safe driver. All the books have been designed to put structure into the learning process, but at the same time they are aimed at ensuring the learner enjoys the process.

In over 90 years of teaching people to drive, BSM instructors have helped millions of people pass their driving test. In my view, *Practice Sessions* is a worthy complement to the best set of books available to help learners become safe drivers and give them a skill which will be for life.

Keith Cameron

Head of Road Safety Policy

Keith Cameron is one of Britain's leading authorities on motoring and driver education. He has held a number of senior positions within the Department of Transport; up to March 1992 he was Chief Driving Examiner with responsibility for all UK driving tests.

Introduction

● *Experience only comes through miles of concentrated practice.*

For many years, The British School of Motoring has recognised the benefit for learner drivers of combining a structured programme of professional tuition with opportunities for supervised private practice. BSM instructors frequently provide informal help to those qualified drivers who choose to help a learner by accompanying them while they practise.

However, the extent to which each individual improves as a result of private practice varies considerably. This is not simply due to the time spent practising, but also to the degree in which the private practice blends with, and is relevant to, the tuition given by a BSM instructor. It is clear that the best results are achieved when a co-operative partnership is formed between all the parties involved.

Government statistics show that newly qualified drivers have a significantly greater chance of having an accident than more experienced drivers. This risk decreases as more miles are driven and more experience

is gained. Professional tuition with a driving instructor is a key part of the learning process — of passing the driving test and developing a higher level of skill as a newly qualified driver — but practice is also essential. When practice is carefully structured, commenced prior to passing the test and is supervised by an experienced driver, the risk of accidents in the early months and years of driving is significantly reduced.

This book is aimed at experienced drivers who wish to assist a learner driver gain experience through practice. However, it is not a driving instruction manual. While the book covers all aspects of the practical driving test, its primary focus is to develop safer driving among newly qualified drivers, not simply to achieve a better chance of the learner passing the practical test. It sets out a framework for a successful four-way partnership between the learner, the accompanying driver, the BSM Centre and the BSM driving instructor.

Practice Sessions explains:
- The roles and responsibilities of the accompanying driver and the learner
- Help that the BSM Centre can provide
- BSM learning resources
- The role of the BSM instructor
- The BSM tuition programme and teaching and assessment methods.

Practice Sessions recommends:
- A structured series of 32 practice sessions, when to undertake them and how to plan them
- Methods to record the learner's progress at practice and communication with the BSM instructor.

Practice Sessions gives advice on:
- Taking the Driving Theory Test
- Taking the Practical Driving Test
- Safe driving after passing the test
- The motoring needs of the newly qualified driver.

● *This book is aimed at experienced drivers...*

Practice Sessions
A guide to accompanying the learner driver

Part 1

Your Role and Responsibilities

We won't fail you

Can You Do It Legally?

Once people decide that they want to learn to drive, they usually can't wait to get started. They are likely to urge you to let them have a go in your car at the earliest opportunity — with you accompanying, of course. But before either of you can take to the public roads together, there are a number of things that will need checking if you want to stay legal. Each is responsible — qualified driver and would-be learner — for ensuring that both of you meet the requirements.

The Learner

■ The minimum age at which a person is allowed to drive a car on the

● *You must be 21 or over to accompany a learner driver.*

public roads is 17, unless you are a disabled person in receipt of mobility allowance, in which case the minimum age is 16
■ Before starting to drive or applying to take the Driving Theory Test, a learner must obtain a provisional driving licence. You can get an application form from any BSM Centre or any Post Office. You may not drive until you have actually received this first licence and signed it in ink
■ Your eyesight must meet the minimum standard.

You, the Accompanying Driver

■ You must have held a full EC/EEA driving licence for the category of vehicle being driven for at least three years
■ You must be at least 21 years of age
■ Unless you are an Approved Driving Instructor (ADI), you are not legally allowed to charge for giving driving lessons or for acting as an accompanying driver
■ It is also an offence to accept money for fuel unless you are an Approved Driving Instructor.

Is Your Car Suitable?

The vehicle must be:

- taxed and the tax disc displayed on the nearside (left) corner of the windscreen
- insured for use by the learner and, of course, for yourself
- fitted with L-plates (D-plates in Wales) of regulation size so that they can be seen from both front and rear. (Do not put L-plates on the windscreen or rear window since they will restrict vision)
- in a roadworthy condition
- If the vehicle is more than three years old it must have an MOT Certificate.

The Practical Requirements

Even as an experienced driver it probably still takes time to get used to driving a different car to your own, since every car feels and handles differently. Bear in mind that, for a learner, this lack of familiarity can be quite alarming and disorientating and it may take them some considerable time to adapt.

At BSM the learner will have their lessons in a Vauxhall Corsa, which will

● *To stay safe, BSM recommends that you fit an extra suction mirror to the windscreen so that you can see behind.*

always be in pristine condition and never more than a few months old. If your car is larger and more powerful than the one in which the learner has their driving lessons, this may cause the learner problems when judging the car's position and when carrying out manoeuvres.

It can also be a problem if the minor controls — such as indicators or windscreen wipers — are positioned in a different place. And if your car suffers minor defects — such as a weak handbrake or a stiff clutch pedal — the learner may struggle.

- Remember to cover up or remove the L-plates when the vehicle is being used by a full-licence holder.

Are You Suitable?

Before you do finally decide to take on the responsibility of accompanying a learner driver there are a number of personal factors that you may find it useful to consider.

Your Own Driving

The learner you accompany will, in all probability, attempt to copy the way you drive, if not while learning, then after passing the test. Nearly all of us have bad habits when driving, some more than others. If you wish to avoid causing the learner problems, it is essential that you take a look at your own driving and ensure that you still keep to the rules and follow the correct procedures.

Conflicts

Depending on how long ago you learnt to drive, you may find that the BSM instructor has taught the learner a different technique or procedure to the one you learned and have probably always used. Advances in technology have to some extent changed experts' views on the safest way to control a car in certain situations.

If you have any doubts or worries, feel free to discuss them with the BSM instructor, who will be happy to explain the reasons behind any differences. You are likely to cause the learner considerable confusion if you start to argue with them or insist that they do something your way. Inevitably, the learner will try to drive exactly as the BSM instructor has taught them.

Patience

To help the learner progress to being a safe driver most effectively, allow the

● *A learner driver will nearly always copy your good example.*

BSM instructor to focus on teaching them each aspect of the syllabus and confine your role to ensuring they have ample opportunity to practise what they have been taught. You are likely to find that even this can be frustrating and requires you to exercise considerable patience.

No two people learn at the same pace; while some learners master co-ordinating the controls with ease, others may take many hours of practice. Similarly, some people have great car control but find it difficult to develop road sense and risk-perception.

Tension will nearly always slow a learner's progress, as will negative criticism that knocks their confidence. If you can make the practice sessions enjoyable, the learner is likely to progress much faster. So do try to be positive, and not fret over how many times the learner gets the same thing wrong. Offer encouragement to try

● *When you are accompanying a learner driver, be prepared to act early to prevent danger developing.*

again, and praise for even the smallest achievement.

You should also show patience with other road users, since they may not always allow for the fact that your car is being driven by a learner.

■ Ensure that you have sufficient time not only to supervise the practice sessions, but also to plan them in advance

■ Give route directions clearly and with plenty of warning in order to give the learner time to react safely.

Your Local BSM Centre

Your local BSM Centre is designed to provide learner drivers with every possible means of help and support as they learn to drive. This support covers

all aspects of the Theory and Practical tests, assists newly qualified drivers to become and remain safe on the roads and offers help with many of their future motoring needs. Each Centre is also able to provide support for the friends and relatives who may wish to be involved in the learner's study, practice and progress.

Most major towns and cities in Great Britain have a BSM Centre and local

BSM instructors operate in all the surrounding areas. So even if you haven't a Centre exactly where you live, you will find a local BSM instructor nearby and your nearest Centre will still be just a phone call away. The ways in which your local Centre can help can be broadly broken down into three areas.

How Your Local Centre can Help

People and Communication

- Each centre is run by a highly trained, friendly team with vast experience of customers and their needs
- It acts as a focal point for the team of BSM Approved Driving Instructors operating in the area, which ensures high quality of instruction, customer care and efficient administration
- It acts as a communication hub with instructors when contact is needed between driving lessons.

Getting Advice and Help

- Advice will be given on appropriate courses of lessons
- Driving assessments can be booked with an instructor, via the Centre, to

● *You can encourage a learner driver to come to a BSM Centre and use its facilities.*

establish the likely number of lessons required and the most appropriate period over which to take them
● Help is provided with applying for a provisional driving licence
● Through the Centre learner drivers can book Theory Tests, Practical Tests, courses of driving lessons, and Mock Practical Driving Tests
● Specialist help for the disabled is available
● Access is also given to BSM insurance services — offering competitive prices and advice especially for new drivers — and to RAC services, which is free for 12 months to all learners buying a minimum of 10 lessons.

Learning Resources at Each Centre
● BSM books and a CD can be purchased
● Free use of PCs is available for all learners who have lessons booked with a BSM instructor, and these may be used to study for the Theory Test and to develop risk awareness
● Advice on post-test training is available, including courses for newly qualified drivers, motorway lessons, parking lessons, night driving, bad-weather driving and advanced driving.
● Many centres are now also equipped with a driving simulator, a state-of-the-art machine unique to BSM and proving ever more popular with customers.

How You Can Help

Sometimes learners are a little nervous about visiting a BSM Centre in order to make use of the facilities. With some, such a visit may involve a difficult journey. Either way, encourage the learner to make the effort, for they will not regret it. You may be able to put them at ease by coming with them on their first visit, as well as help with any transport problems... and you are always very welcome at any Centre.

BSM Learning Resources

The BSM Approved Driving Instructor

The BSM instructor is, of course, the learner's most valuable learning resource of all. All driving instructors are required to pass a rigorous examination conducted by the Driving Standards Agency in order to gain entry to the register of Approved Driving Instructors.

This requires considerable training and, at BSM, we pride ourselves on providing by far the best and most comprehensive such training courses anywhere in the world. The friendly, caring and professional manner of these experts instills confidence and breeds success in learners.

Learners have lessons with an instructor suited to their particular needs, something we consider essential if good progress is to be made. If, for instance, a learner prefers to learn with a female instructor, the BSM Centre team will do their best to make this happen.

After a learner's first lesson, the Centre staff always telephone to see if the learner was happy with everything.

The BSM Books and CD Rom

Pass Your Driving Theory Test

- A step-by-step guide to the driving Theory Test
- Covers all the topics contained in the Theory Test
- Provides clear and precise information about what a candidate needs to know
- Contains exercises and questions to test a learner's knowledge
- Prepares learners for driving on today's crowded roads
- With over 200 fun illustrations to

help illustrate the facts
- Available at BSM Centres and all good bookshops
- See also 'Studying for the Theory Test' on pages 26–31.

Driving Theory Test Questions
- Contains all the Driving Standards Agency questions that can be asked in the Theory Test from the new enlarged question bank
- Allows learners to test themselves on their driving theory knowledge
- Answers to each question at the end of every topic with explanations where appropriate

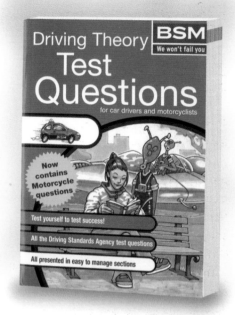

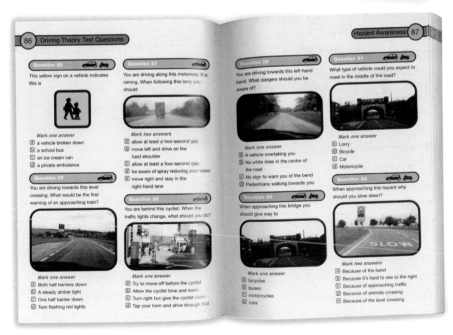

- Colour-coded bars allow instant location of topics for revision purposes
- Complements the Theory Test text book — *Pass Your Driving Theory Test*
- Available at BSM Centres and all good bookshops
- See also 'Studying for the Theory Test' on pages 26–31.

learner is told whether they passed or failed

- See also 'Studying for the Theory Test' on pages 26–31.

Driving Theory Test Questions CD Rom

- Contains all the questions and information in the book of the same title above
- Either: Work through questions on a topic-by-topic basis and after each question the answer selected will be shown as right or wrong, with an explanation where appropriate
- Or: Choose the random question option and select how many questions to answer. At the end the

● *Fun illustrations lighten the learning load and help learners remember the facts.*

Pass Your Driving Test

- A step-by-step guide to the Practical Driving Test
- Covers all the topics and skills that can be included in the test
- Contains tips from expert driving instructors and examiners
- Introduces safe driving habits
- With over 200 fun illustrations to help remember the facts
- Available at BSM Centres and all good bookshops.

The BSM Interactive Computers

The Question Bank

Available free at BSM Centres to all learners who have lessons booked with a BSM instructor.

The Interactive Challenge

- Being able to recognise potential hazards forms an important part of the Driving Test
- Road users who are not aware of what is going on around them may make mistakes that could turn into serious accidents
- The Interactive Challenge gives a driver's eye view of dangerous driving situations
- Using real-time video footage, you are asked to spot potential hazards
- After each section you are given a percentage score and helpful hints
- A unique BSM programme and a Prince Michael of Kent Road Safety Award winner, 1999–2000
- The Driving Standards Agency is currently developing video hazard perception exercises to include in future versions of the Theory Test.

● *The BSM simulator is just like the real thing. After getting in and belting up, you are ready to take to the virtual road in your virtual Corsa.*

The BSM Driving Simulator

The BSM driving simulator is now available at more than half of BSM Centres. The simulator is the latest in driver-training technology designed specifically with learners in mind. It feels and handles just like a real car, only instead of windows and mirrors there are three computer screens — and the controls are exactly the same as the Vauxhall Corsa, the BSM training car.

■ Since no licence is required, learners can start to learn before they are 17
■ Learners may practise on their own, at their own pace, without embarrassment at being watched
■ Anyone feeling nervous about getting started is likely to benefit
■ The same situation can be repeated as often as needed until confidence is gained. This is not always possible on a public road
■ Learners can make errors without any stress or danger.

The Novice Simulator Course

This six-hour course — normally split into two or three sessions — covers the basic driving skills. The first five hours are on the simulator, followed by a lesson with a BSM instructor in a BSM training car. Topics covered include:

● *Even learner drivers can practise safe motorway driving in the simulator.*

- cockpit drill and safety checks
- starting and stopping the engine
- moving off and stopping on the level and up and down hill
- steering
- changing up and down through all the gears
- manoeuvring at slow speeds
- accelerating and braking
- turning left and right
- emergency stops.

The simulator automatically adjusts the amount of help given to match what the learner gets right and wrong.

On completion of the five hours, most people find their first lesson in a car with the BSM instructor to be very rewarding. Now that they can use the controls, they can concentrate on what is going on around them rather than on what they are doing with their hands and feet.

The Motorway Simulator Course
For details of the motorway course see pages 150–152.

Practice Sessions
A guide to accompanying the learner driver

Part	The Learning Process
2	Explained

Studying for the Theory Test

Since 1 July 1996 the driving test has been split into two parts, a Theory Test of multiple-choice questions and a Practical Test of the candidate's driving. Learners must pass both parts before they can obtain a full driving licence. Learners must pass the Theory Test before they can apply for the Practical Test. Your local BSM Centre can provide details of the most convenient Theory Test centre and can help with booking the test.

Special provisions are available for non-English speaking people and those with special needs. Full details can be obtained from your local BSM Centre.

The Theory Test is conducted on a computer using a touch-screen. The test contains 35 questions chosen from a question bank of over 1,000. In order to pass, a minimum of 30 must be answered correctly. Each of the 35 questions in the test will appear on the screen in turn. The correct answer is selected by touching the screen. The candidate can move backwards and forwards through the questions and may also flag up questions they want to look at again later in the test. Most questions ask for one correct answer to be selected from a choice of four possibilities.

● *Most people find it best to study the theory and start having driving lessons at the same time.*

● *For some learners, answering the questions is a hurdle, usually because of insufficient study...*

Some questions ask for two or more answers to be selected as correct from a longer list. The test lasts for 40 minutes and the time remaining is displayed on the screen. Most people have little problem answering all the questions in the time available but, for some, getting 30 correct is a huge hurdle, usually because of inappropriate or insufficient study.

The result is normally available within 30 minutes of taking the test. If the learner passes, your local BSM Centre can provide assistance with booking the Practical Test. Should they fail, they must wait a minimum of three clear working days before taking the Theory Test again.

Since no two people are the same, each learner needs to decide for themselves how they wish to go about studying for the Theory Test. Some people prefer to get the theory under their belt first before starting driving lessons. This is fine, but for many people it feels too much like academic hard graft, since there is no chance to link the theory to the practice. Most people seem to find it easier to study the theory and start driving lessons at the same time. The chance to put some of the theory into practice makes the theory feel more relevant and understandable.

Any learner who chooses to study in this way at BSM can benefit from the experience and expert guidance of their BSM instructor to help achieve success at both parts of the test. In addition, learners at BSM are offered a unique range of BSM materials and learning aids, all designed to make learning as easy as possible for every type and age of learner. Even people who have never passed an examination in their lives, those who have learning difficulties or those who have had no experience of studying for many years, can be confident of receiving the right sort of help at BSM and achieve a Theory Test pass.

The Range of BSM Theory Test Services

The BSM instructor will make links between the theory topics and the actual skills being practised in the tuition car. Where necessary, the instructor will help the learner devise a study plan and, of course, answer any queries that may arise about the Theory Test questions.

For Private Study at Home

Pass Your Driving Theory Test
This BSM book is packed with information to help understand the safety issues that lie behind the questions in the Theory Test, exercises to help thinking and examination techniques, quizzes to test knowledge, and example Theory Test questions. See page 18 for more detail.

Driving Theory Test Questions
This BSM book contains all the Driving Standards Agency Theory Test Questions for both cars and motorcycles. Presented in easy-to-manage sections, it also includes all the correct answers. See page 19 for more detail.

Driving Theory Test Questions CD-ROM
A BSM CD-Rom version of the book. See page 20 for more detail.

For Study at any BSM Centre

The BSM Touch-screen Computers

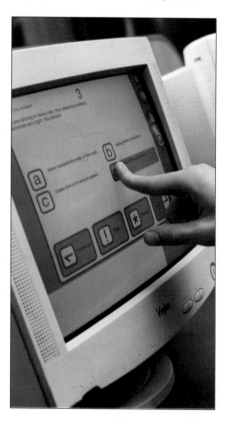

This is a free service offered to all learners who have booked driving lessons with a BSM instructor.

The learner can practise answering any or all of the Theory Test questions either by topic or in random sequences. Most importantly, they can do so using the PC touch-screen in exactly the same way as they will when they take the real examination at a Driving Standards Agency Approved Theory Test Centre. This service is unique to BSM, allowing the learner to experience realistic examination conditions and greatly helping to remove test nerves on the actual day.

The Study Guide

The Study Guide for the Theory Test is a very efficient PC-based method to help a learner learn all they need to know to pass the Theory Test. It is unique to BSM and can only be accessed at a BSM Centre. The Study Guide can be used to learn the whole syllabus in easy stages, or to select particular categories for study or revision. When a section is selected for study, the learner will, for no more than a couple of minutes at a time:

- listen to a series of short statements
- read the same statements on screen
- see the picture or road signs where appropriate.

In doing this, the learner will have heard, read and seen all the information needed to answer all the actual Theory Test questions on that topic correctly. Listening, reading and visualising at the same time is a

proven way of retaining information quickly and easily. The learner is then invited to test themselves on all the real Theory Test questions which relate to the information they have just learnt.

Helping the Learner

At home, you can help by ensuring that the learner has suitable learning resources to help their study and devotes sufficient time to learn what is needed. You can also help by testing them, and even by working through some of the materials together.

Your most valuable contribution to their study for the Theory Test may well be to encourage them to visit their BSM Centre frequently and make the most of its resources.

Theory Test Syllabus

Alertness:

Observation, anticipation, concentration, awareness, distraction, boredom.

Attitude:

Consideration, close following, courtesy, priority.

● *Ensure the learner devotes sufficient time to study what is needed to achieve a pass.*

Safety and your vehicle:

Fault detection, defects and their effects on safety, use of safety equipment, emissions, noise.

Safety margins:

Stopping distances, road surfaces, skidding, weather conditions.

Hazard awareness:

Anticipation, hazard awareness, attention, speed and distance, reaction time, the effects of alcohol and drugs, tiredness.

Vulnerable road users:

Pedestrians, children, elderly drivers, disabled people, cyclists, motorcyclists, animals, new drivers.

Other types of vehicle:

Motorcycles, lorries, buses.

Vehicle handling:

Weather conditions, road conditions, time of day, speed, traffic calming.

Motorway rules:

Speed limits, lane discipline, stopping, lighting, parking.

Rules of the road:

Speed limits, lane discipline, parking, lighting.

Road and traffic signs:

Road signs, speed limits, road markings, regulations.

Documents:

Licences, insurance, MOT test certificate.

Accidents:

First aid, warning devices, reporting procedures, safety regulations.

Vehicle loading:

Stability, towing regulations.

BSM—A Programme of Tuition

Most of us only have a fairly hazy memory of exactly how we learnt to drive and the difficulties we may have experienced. This is especially true if we have held a full licence for many years. For some of us the experience was traumatic, confusing and sometimes embarrassing. Most of our friends, and especially our male friends, claim to have found learning to drive very easy and assure us they passed their driving test first time after little or no professional tuition. And what tuition they did have is often described as involving little more than the opportunity to practise legally.

People's memories have a habit of playing tricks, of recalling the good and conveniently burying past problems in some deep recess of the

● *'I'm much better than you are... at crashing?'*

mind. In a similar way, 98% of qualified drivers questioned in an insurance company survey claimed that their own driving was better and safer than average. You don't have to be a statistical genius to suggest that some of them must be wrong.

Driving Today

Whatever our own memories of learning to drive, it is clear that circumstances are now different. To drive safely on today's roads requires a higher standard of competence than has historically been the case, and the standard required to pass the driving test has increased somewhat to reflect this. Modern traffic conditions are perhaps of more consequence, as they make it more difficult to drive without committing errors; the test would still be harder to pass even had the standard remained exactly the same.

The BSM Solution

Fortunately, not all the news is negative. Over the last decade or

more, BSM has led the way in developing far more efficient ways of teaching people to drive. One such development has been the creation of a logical sequence and progression of lessons that can be tailored to suit individual needs. Every learner who has driving lessons with a BSM

● *A personal programme of tuition is agreed with every learner.*

instructor is now provided with a personal, planned programme of tuition. This programme is agreed with the learner and takes account not only of any previous driving experience they may have, but also their own preferred style of learning and level of confidence. It aims to prepare each learner for the driving test and beyond, at a pace that maintains motivation by allowing maximum progress on each lesson without going too far too fast and destroying confidence. The result is that more learners now enjoy their driving lessons and look forward to the next one.

The BSM Track Record

This satisfying and pleasurable experience is further enhanced by the BSM system of assessing and recording each learner's progress. A learner's ability and motivation to learn are greatly enhanced when they are invited to share in the process of assessing their progress with their BSM instructor. In doing so, they start to perceive their own strengths and weaknesses and are able to plan their next step forward with their instructor. The degree to which a learner has progressed is recorded on their BSM Track record, a section of which is shown on the next page.

How You Can Help

■ Use the BSM Track Record to keep yourself aware of the learner's progress at the different driving skills recorded, especially if you have no chance to speak to their BSM instructor

■ The Track Record can help you judge the learner's likely level of performance when they practise with you so that you are less likely to expect too much or too little from them

■ A glance at the Track Record will help you plan a route of suitable difficulty for their practice session.

● Above, the cover of Track Record and, right, the four Track Record assessment pages.

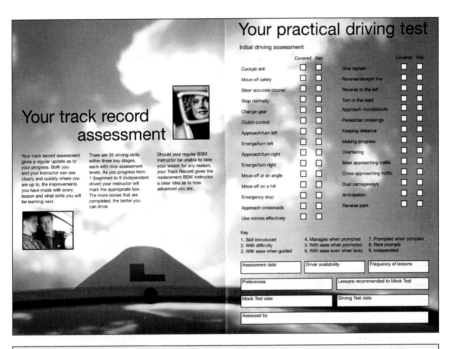

Your track record assessment

Your track record assessment gives a regular update as to your progress. Both you and your instructor can see clearly and quickly where you are up to, the improvements you have made with every lesson and what skills you will be learning next.

There are 35 driving skills within three key stages, each with nine assessment levels. As you progress from 1 (beginner) to 9 (independent driver) your instructor will mark the appropriate box. The more boxes that are completed, the better you can drive.

Should your regular BSM instructor be unable to take your lesson for any reason, your Track Record gives the replacement BSM instructor a clear idea as to how advanced you are.

Your practical driving test

Initial driving assessment

	Covered	Key		Covered	Key
Cockpit drill	☐	☐	Give signals	☐	☐
Move off safely	☐	☐	Reverse/straight line	☐	☐
Steer accurate course	☐	☐	Reverse to the left	☐	☐
Stop normally	☐	☐	Turn in the road	☐	☐
Change gear	☐	☐	Approach roundabouts	☐	☐
Clutch control	☐	☐	Pedestrian crossings	☐	☐
Approach/turn left	☐	☐	Keeping distance	☐	☐
Emerge/turn left	☐	☐	Making progress	☐	☐
Approach/turn right	☐	☐	Overtaking	☐	☐
Emerge/turn right	☐	☐	Meet approaching traffic	☐	☐
Move off at an angle	☐	☐	Cross approaching traffic	☐	☐
Move off on a hill	☐	☐	Dual carriageways	☐	☐
Emergency stop	☐	☐	Anticipation	☐	☐
Approach crossroads	☐	☐	Reverse park	☐	☐
Use mirrors effectively	☐	☐			

Key
1. Skill introduced
2. With difficulty
3. With ease when guided
4. Manages when prompted
5. With ease when prompted
6. With ease even when busy
7. Prompted when complex
8. Rare prompts
9. Independent

Assessment date	Driver availability	Frequency of lessons
Preferences		Lessons recommended to Mock Test
Mock Test date		Driving Test date
Assessed by		

Your instructor's assessment

Key Stage 1

	1	2	3	4	5	6	7	8	9
Carry out cockpit drill	☐	☐	☐	☐	☐	☐	☐	☐	☐
Move off safely	☐	☐	☐	☐	☐	☐	☐	☐	☐
Stop normally	☐	☐	☐	☐	☐	☐	☐	☐	☐
Change gear	☐	☐	☐	☐	☐	☐	☐	☐	☐
Use clutch control	☐	☐	☐	☐	☐	☐	☐	☐	☐
Approach and turn left	☐	☐	☐	☐	☐	☐	☐	☐	☐
Approach and emerge left	☐	☐	☐	☐	☐	☐	☐	☐	☐
Approach and turn right	☐	☐	☐	☐	☐	☐	☐	☐	☐
Approach and emerge right	☐	☐	☐	☐	☐	☐	☐	☐	☐
Move off at an angle	☐	☐	☐	☐	☐	☐	☐	☐	☐
Move off on a hill	☐	☐	☐	☐	☐	☐	☐	☐	☐
Stop in an emergency	☐	☐	☐	☐	☐	☐	☐	☐	☐
Approach crossroads	☐	☐	☐	☐	☐	☐	☐	☐	☐

Key Stage 2

	1	2	3	4	5	6	7	8	9
Use mirrors effectively	☐	☐	☐	☐	☐	☐	☐	☐	☐
Give signals	☐	☐	☐	☐	☐	☐	☐	☐	☐
Reverse in a straight line	☐	☐	☐	☐	☐	☐	☐	☐	☐
Reverse to the left	☐	☐	☐	☐	☐	☐	☐	☐	☐
Reverse to the right	☐	☐	☐	☐	☐	☐	☐	☐	☐

	1	2	3	4	5	6	7	8	9
Turn the car in the road	☐	☐	☐	☐	☐	☐	☐	☐	☐
Deal with one-way systems	☐	☐	☐	☐	☐	☐	☐	☐	☐
Approach roundabouts	☐	☐	☐	☐	☐	☐	☐	☐	☐
Deal with pedestrian crossings	☐	☐	☐	☐	☐	☐	☐	☐	☐
Approach complex junctions	☐	☐	☐	☐	☐	☐	☐	☐	☐
Keep space from traffic	☐	☐	☐	☐	☐	☐	☐	☐	☐
Keep pace with traffic	☐	☐	☐	☐	☐	☐	☐	☐	☐
Overtake traffic	☐	☐	☐	☐	☐	☐	☐	☐	☐
Meet traffic	☐	☐	☐	☐	☐	☐	☐	☐	☐
Cross traffic	☐	☐	☐	☐	☐	☐	☐	☐	☐
Deal with dual carriageways	☐	☐	☐	☐	☐	☐	☐	☐	☐
Anticipate other traffic	☐	☐	☐	☐	☐	☐	☐	☐	☐
Reverse park	☐	☐	☐	☐	☐	☐	☐	☐	☐

Key Stage 3

	1	2	3	4	5	6	7	8	9
Drive on direction only	☐	☐	☐	☐	☐	☐	☐	☐	☐
Assess risk accurately	☐	☐	☐	☐	☐	☐	☐	☐	☐
Use visual search skills	☐	☐	☐	☐	☐	☐	☐	☐	☐

Key
1. Skill introduced
2. With difficulty
3. With ease when guided
4. Manages when prompted
5. With ease when prompted
6. With ease even when busy
7. Prompted when complex
8. Rare prompts
9. Independent

The Structure of a BSM Driving Lesson

Quality of Instruction

For a number of years, the quality of instruction given by ADIs has been steadily improving. The entry examinations to the profession have become much harder and, certainly at BSM, driving instructors not only receive much more in-depth training at the start of their careers, but also significant ongoing professional development training at regular intervals thereafter.

The somewhat haphazard teaching style of driving lessons in earlier years has been replaced by far more structured lessons for learners, which in many respects follow the same pattern used in formal education by schoolteachers and lecturers.

How You Can Help

You intend to accompany a learner driver and keep them safe and legal while they practise what they have been taught in their lessons with their BSM driving instructor. The more you understand of how they are taught, the more valuable you are likely to make their practice.

You are not reading this book in order to become a driving instructor — although the experience of accompanying a learner might just make you consider a new career. However, reading the following explanation of a lesson structure should give you a small insight into what makes a good driving lesson. As a result, you will find it easier to

● *Once haphazard, today's teaching style in lessons is more structured...*

understand the way in which the Recommended Practice Sessions are constructed and the reasons behind the practice methods that are proposed.

Lesson Structure

Recap

A recap takes place at the very beginning of a lesson and may be used to:

- remind the learner what has been learnt so far
- check what the learner remembers from previous lessons, particularly knowledge and skills that they will need in this lesson
- put the current lesson into context

- *'I'm sure my instructor told me to keep to the right...'*

- find out the experience and knowledge of a learner being seen for the first time
- find out the result of any practice undertaken since the last lesson.

It will normally involve asking a few questions and giving reminders to the learner where necessary.

This is what you will be doing at the start of each practice session with the learner when you ascertain what they remember their instructor has taught them about the skill they are about to practise.

Objective

An objective tells the learner what the instructor intends to teach during that lesson. It should spell out exactly what the learner will know and be able to do by the end of the lesson that they do not know or cannot do at the beginning. Ideally, the objective should state:

- what is to be learned and why
- how the instructor intends to make this happen
- what will be achieved by the end of the lesson.

> This is what you will be doing at the start of each practice session with the learner when you explain what is to be practised and how.

- *This is called a 'briefing'.*

Briefing

Before a learner can practise a skill effectively, they need to know what to do, how to do it, when to do it and why. When an instructor explains this to a learner it is called a 'briefing'. The learner does not need to know all there is to know about the topic in order to start practising, only the main points needed to get them started. The instructor's ability to keep an explanation short and simple, without leaving out any essential pieces of information, is crucial to the learner's success.

> When you accompany a learner driver you will not need to give a briefing because the BSM instructor will already have done this on the driving lesson. However, the questions you ask in the recap may reveal gaps in the learner's memory or understanding of what has been taught. In this case you may be able to remind the learner from your own knowledge and experience, or look up the information in one of the BSM books. If neither is possible, it is best to consult with the BSM instructor or local Centre before continuing with further practice.

Demonstrations

BSM instructors make use of demonstrations in several different ways. Properly used, a demonstration can drastically reduce the amount of explanation needed; it can also make it easy for learners to see what they are trying to achieve or where they go wrong. BSM instructors may also give a form of demonstration from the passenger seat. For example, they may demonstrate visual searching skills by pointing out the hazards, as they occur, that they would be paying most attention to if they were actually driving.

When you accompany a learner driver on a practice session you should not need to give any formal demonstration. The BSM instructor will have done this, if appropriate, during the learner's driving lesson. But do bear in mind that when the learner sees you drive, they will watch what you are doing as though it were a demonstration. Take care not to teach bad habits. You may wish to demonstrate from the passenger seat, particularly in Recommended Practice Sessions 29 and 30, Assessing Risks and Commentary Driving.

● *The learner may well copy you, so take care not to teach them bad habits.*

Practice

Practice can be seen, in many ways, as the most important part of every driving lesson. Nearly every driving lesson is likely to be devoted 70% to practice. A BSM instructor will take great care to ensure that the practice is relevant to the lesson objective and that a suitable area and route is chosen. They will also decide exactly how difficult the practice should be and, most crucially, how much help to give.

In very general terms, when learners practise a skill for the first few times the BSM instructor will guide them closely by talking them through everything they have to do, as they do it. Next, the learner will be encouraged to practise the skill with less help, only being prompted and reminded as needed. Finally, the learner will be encouraged to perform the skill and make decisions without help. This is the start of the independence that all learners must achieve before they can drive safely on their own.

Further Practice

If the BSM instructor is teaching the learner a new driving skill, they are likely to need several practice attempts before any great progress is made.

During these attempts, the instructor will have spotted faults and corrected some of them. In order to teach the learner effectively, the instructor must not only spot any faults, but also analyse what caused them. At some stage in this process, the instructor is likely to park and explain what still needs to be improved. The instructor will suggest a remedy — that is, a way of the learner improving. Further practice will normally follow, either of the whole skill, or of the specific items that require improvement.

It is hoped that this brief account of the complex process of practice and further practice will help you see the importance of working in partnership with the BSM instructor when you accompany a learner driver. Unless you are aware of the stage a learner has reached in this process and the remedies that have been proposed by the BSM instructor to improve any faults, you will not really be in a position to ensure that how and what the learner practises will be beneficial.

● *'Your steering's a bit wonky but you applied the handbrake just wonderfully...'*

Summary

At the end of every driving lesson, the BSM instructor will provide the learner with a brief summary of what has and hasn't been achieved. At the start of the lesson, the learner will have been set an objective to achieve by the end of the lesson, and will then want to know the extent to which they have achieved this objective. This involves:

● a mixture of praise and constructive criticism

● agreement with the learner about the points made

● completion of the learner Track Record

● recommending private practice sessions and recording suggestions and comments

● telling the learner what they will learn on their next lesson.

Before you accompany a learner for a practice session you will need to look at the Track Record and the Recommended Practice Session Forms at the back of this book. It is only in this way that you can plan a constructive session. You will assist the learner if you also summarise how they got on whilst practising and record any comments for the benefit of their BSM instructor.

Helping a Learner to Practise

The Four-Way Partnership

By far the most effective way to help a learner driver pass their driving test and become a safe driver is to actively develop a four-way circular partnership:

You — The Learner — The BSM Centre — The BSM Driving Instructor

This enables each party involved to take appropriate responsibility for the learner's success and safety.

You will do your best to accompany the learner on practice sessions as often as possible and follow the recommendations given by the BSM instructor. You will briefly record that the practice took place, any major faults you may have noticed and what skills improved.

The learner will take responsibility for making sure that both you and their instructor have access to the Track Record and Practice Record. The learner will make use of the BSM Centre resources where possible and commit themselves to periods of home study.

● *The four-way partnership, a circle of success.*

The **BSM Centre** can organise administration and bookings for lessons and tests. It can provide the full range of BSM learning resources for the learner. It can act, when necessary, as an information hub so that all parties are kept informed.

The **BSM instructor** will create an individual teaching strategy and course of lessons based on the learner's needs and ability. They will teach all aspects of the syllabus to the learner, for all topics related to the driving test and for safe driving as a qualified driver, following the guidelines laid down by the Driving Standards Agency. They will advise you and the learner which practice sessions are appropriate and when, as well as recording progress in the Track Record.

When to Start Accompanying a Learner Driver

The BSM instructor will advise you when to start accompanying the learner on practice sessions. To a certain extent, this will depend on the ability of the learner, their level of confidence and your own, the type of car they will practise in and local geography.

In general terms, both the Driving Standards Agency and BSM advise not to start practising too early. A bad experience can destroy your confidence or that of the learner. It is certainly best to wait until the learner has a reasonable ability to use the basic controls. You may easily create danger if the learner cannot move off, accelerate, brake and steer with reasonable fluency. All BSM tuition cars are fitted with dual controls, which makes the essential task of learning car control much safer than in a private vehicle.

Where to Allow the Learner to Practise

Each of the 32 BSM Recommended Practice Sessions which follow in the next section suggests the type of road, route and traffic conditions that are likely to be appropriate. The BSM instructor is likely to have extensive local knowledge of your area and will often suggest suitable places to practise either to the learner or to yourself.

Do remember that in the early stages of learning to drive, the learner may need you to drive them somewhere safe and suitable before you change seats and let them behind the wheel to practise.

Leaving Things to the Experts

Stick by the general rule that it is best to leave the BSM instructor to take responsibility for all that is taught to the learner. Your task is to create safe and legal opportunities for the learner to practise what they have been taught.

For safety reasons, there are two specific skills which BSM suggests should be left entirely to the BSM driving instructor:

■ Emergency Stops — obviously the learner may encounter a real life situation while practising that requires them to stop in an

● *It is best to leave some things — like emergency stops — to the experts.*

emergency. However, practising this on a public road, purely to gain experience for the test, can be dangerous and is best left to be taught by and practised with the professional

■ Motorway driving — learner drivers are not, of course, allowed on the motorway. However, when they have passed their test, the newly qualified driver's first trip down a motorway can be quite alarming. See pages 150–152 for BSM's suggested action.

The BSM Recommended Practice System

The BSM Recommended Practice System consists of 32 practice sessions each of which is carefully graded and structured. Each practice session is designed to complement the professional driving lessons in which the BSM instructor will teach the learner specific skills. Each practice session includes suggestions for more advanced practice once the learner has mastered the basic skill. The BSM instructor will advise the learner which of these advanced exercises are appropriate and when to try them.

Each Practice Session follows the same structure and includes the following sections:

- The skill or skills to be practised
- When and where to practise
- General safety considerations
- A note on stating the objective
- Ways of checking the learner's knowledge of the topic
- Major points to check during practice
- Suggested advanced exercises
- Common problems.

At the end of each practice session it is very helpful to both the learner and their BSM driving instructor if you:

- Discuss how things went with the learner and see if you can both agree about what went well and what went badly
- Record details of the practice session in the spaces provided

● *The more of each, the better...*

towards the back of this book
- Make brief comments about progress or problems that you feel the BSM instructor needs to be aware of.

Do not hesitate to contact either your local BSM Centre or the learner's BSM driving instructor if you have any serious worries about the learner's performance or progress, or if either of you have any doubts about correct driving procedures or other related queries.

Contents of Recommended Practice Sessions

Practice Sessions

A guide to accompanying the learner driver

Part
3

**The 32 BSM Recommended
Practice Sessions**

Session 1
Moving Off and Stopping on a Level Surface

Where and When to Practise

Ideally for the first few practices you need a large, flat, empty car park, or a long, straight, level road, which is fairly wide with little traffic and not too many parked cars. Remember that unless the BSM instructor has already taught the learner how to turn left, you may need to change seats with the learner in order to turn the car round and then allow practice in the opposite direction.

Changing seats too often can be frustrating and time consuming, particularly if the seat position and mirrors need to be adjusted each time you swap. For this reason, BSM recommend that you do not attempt this practice too early if you cannot find a suitable road or car park.

General Safety

- Avoid any road where children are playing
- Personally check that it is safe before moving off
  - Make sure you are a reasonable distance from any car parked ahead of you. It should only be necessary to steer very slightly in order to reach the normal driving position
  - When parking, take control of the steering wheel if necessary rather than allow your tyres to risk damage by hitting the kerb.

● *Changing seats too often can be frustrating.*

Explain What Is to Be Practised and How

Check Knowledge and Understanding

Ask a few questions to check that the learner can remember what their BSM instructor has taught them about moving off. (See *Pass Your Driving Test*, pages 28–33.)

Major Points to Check During Practice

- Carries out 'The Cockpit Drill' — doors, seat, steering, seat-belt, mirrors (DSSSM) — correctly, in sequence and reasonably quickly
- Completes safety checks before starting engine in correct sequence

● *Take control of the steering wheel if necessary rather than hit the kerb.*

- Prepares the controls of the car to be ready to move — correct gear, adequate gas, clutch at biting point and handbrake
- Observes to check it is safe, including blindspot check
- Signals if necessary
- Co-ordinates the controls smoothly as the car starts to move
- Steers adequately
- Assumes normal driving position
- Chooses a safe place to stop
- Uses Mirror, Signal, Manoeuvre (MSM) when stopping
- Brakes gently to a stop
- Positions accurately when stopped, and reasonably close to the kerb.

Advanced Exercises

(a) Remain on a quiet road. Use a stopwatch to time each move away and try and speed the process without any loss of control or observation. This will help when on busy roads.

(b) Move off with the radio on so that you cannot hear the sound of the engine change when the clutch reaches biting point. This will help where other traffic noise drowns the sound of your engine.

(c) Move off on slightly busier roads, practising selecting the first safe gap in the traffic.

(d) Move off at traffic lights.

Common Problems

Stalling:
- Lets the clutch up too far
- Sets too little gas
- Eases off the gas as the clutch comes up
- Does not keep feet still
- Releases the handbrake too late
- Kangaroo hops as the car moves off
- Feels pressure to move off quickly and loses confidence.

Stopping:
- Finds difficulty braking and steering to stop accurately
- Is unable to judge distance from the kerb
- Jolts as the car stops.

Observation:
- Takes too long between looking and moving
- Makes no blindspot check
- Uses the Mirror Signal Manoeuvre sequence incorrectly.

- *A common problem is stalling because the clutch is let up too far.*

Session 2

Using the Steering Wheel

There are two aspects of steering that should be practised:

(1) Steering in a straight line or to keep a normal driving position on the road. This should normally only require very slight movements of the steering wheel.

(2) Steering to turn a corner or manoeuvre. In this case, the steering wheel will need to be turned much further, perhaps even to full lock in one direction and then full lock in the other direction.

The first aspect can initially be practised on a quiet, reasonably straight road. The second can first be practised in an empty car park.

BSM recommend that their learners master the 'pull-push' steering method (illustrated on the right), because once they have achieved this, they tend to find the steering required when turning corners and completing manoeuvres causes few problems. You may need to check that you understand the

● *Turning Left — slide left hand to the top of the wheel.*

● *Grip and pull down with the left hand while sliding the right hand down.*

● *Grip and push up with the right hand while sliding up the left hand.*

● *Grip and pull down with the left hand while sliding the right hand down.*

● *Repeat as necessary.*

● *Turning Right — start the above with your right hand.*

method and can do it yourself before you supervise your learner's practice session.

General Safety

■ Some people find it difficult to steer in a straight line. Be ready to take control of the steering wheel should the need arise

■ Having turned the steering wheel in one direction, learners often forget that they need to turn the wheel back in the opposite direction in order to straighten up. Prompt them the moment you feel they are leaving things too late

● Only practise 'pull-push' steering at slow speeds, with little or no gas, or using clutch control to keep the car slow.

Explain What Is to Be Practised and How

Check Knowledge and Understanding

Ask a few questions to ensure that the learner remembers what their BSM instructor has taught them about steering in a straight line and 'pull-push' steering. Ask the BSM instructor to demonstrate the method if you are unsure. (See *Pass Your Driving Test*, pages 25 and 27.)

● *Some people find it difficult to steer in a straight line.*

- Carries out the Cockpit Drill correctly. The correct seating position is essential in order to steer easily
- Completes safety checks before starting the engine
- Makes adequate observations to check it is safe to move off
- Gives a signal if necessary
- Keeps speed under control
- Looks well ahead and not at the bonnet or the controls
- Does not steer when the car is stopped, which can damage the tyres
- Uses smooth 'pull-push' steering with both hands on the wheel
- Keeps both hands on the steering wheel, holding it in a suitable position
- Turns the wheel back after steering, at the correct time
- Does not cross hands on the steering wheel.

Advanced Exercises

If you live near a suitable off-road centre you may be able to practise steering through slaloms. Alternatively you could book a lesson on a BSM simulator if one is available near to you.

Common Problems

- Looks at the bonnet or controls and causes erratic steering
- Makes small movements of the steering wheel when large 'pull-push' movements are needed
- Steers too much or too late
- Corrects the steering too late or not at all
- Rests right elbow on the window ledge
- Wobbles when changing gear
- Lets the steering wheel spin back.

● *Make sure the learner keeps both hands on the steering wheel.*

Session 3
Clutch Control

Where and When to Practise

Find a quiet, reasonably straight, level road with not too many parked cars. The learner is going to practise clutch control in the way shown to them by their BSM instructor. This involves making the car creep forwards as slowly as possible for a few metres and stopping again at a pre-selected point. You need to select a marker, such as a lamp-post, by which to stop the front wheels.

General Safety

- Avoid any road where children may be playing
- Most of the learner's attention is likely to be focused on the clutch, so keep looking all around to ensure it is safe
- Keep a reasonable distance from the kerb and avoid driving in the gutter; the bumps will make it harder to control the car
- Do not allow the engine to over-rev for long periods of time
- Do not practise for too long at a time without a break, since the clutch might overheat
- If you do smell the clutch burning, turn off the engine and wait at least ten minutes.

Explain What Is to Be Practised and How

The object of the exercise is to make the car move very slowly under clutch control and to stop at exact points without stalling.

Check Knowledge and Understanding

Ask a few questions to ensure that the learner remembers what their BSM instructor has taught them about how the clutch works and what is happening when they use the clutch pedal. Also check that they know in which driving situations clutch control is essential. (See *Pass Your Driving Test*, pages 23 and 26.)

Major Points to Check During Practice

■ Completes Cockpit Drill and safety checks before starting the engine
■ Selects correct gear
■ Sets sufficient gas
■ Finds clutch biting point
■ Co-ordinates releasing the handbrake
■ Carries out adequate observations
■ Can control the clutch to creep forwards and stop
■ Stops accurately
■ Makes the car safe.

Advanced Exercises

(a) Try exactly the same practice but facing uphill.
(b) Practise in simple driving situations where there are queues of traffic and it is necessary to keep creeping forward and stopping.
(c) Imagine there is a parked car close in front; practise clutch control and steering briskly to move away around it.
(d) Highlight clutch control when practising other exercises that require it, such as manoeuvres and emerging from junctions.

Common Problems

■ Stalls due to easing off the gas pedal
■ Does not keep foot still on the clutch
■ Unable to keep a very slow speed due to too much clutch movement
■ Loses control of the clutch when trying to steer sharply at the same time.

How the Clutch Works

The same principles apply in a front-wheel-drive car.

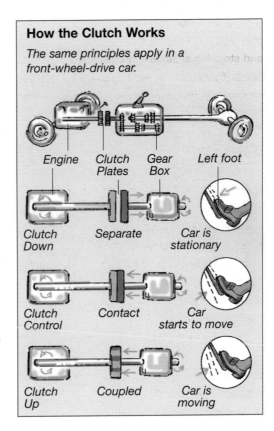

Engine   Clutch   Gear   Left foot
          Plates   Box

Clutch   Separate   Car is
Down   stationary

Clutch   Contact   Car
Control   starts to move

Clutch   Coupled   Car is
Up   moving

Session 4

Moving Off and Stopping Uphill

Where and When to Practise

Find a quiet, reasonably wide road with ideally a fairly long and gentle uphill slope and not too many parked cars. Park just after the bottom of the hill, facing up it.

General Safety

- Avoid any road where children are playing
- Personally check that it is safe before moving off
- Do not allow the learner to over-rev the engine for any length of time
- Keep an eye on the temperature gauge if practising for any length of time
- Allow the clutch to cool down between practices if biting

● *If you smell the clutch burning, stop practising for at least ten minutes.*

point is held for too long
- Stop practising for at least ten minutes if you overheat the clutch.

Explain What Is to Be Practised and How

Check Knowledge and Understanding

Ask a few questions to ensure the learner remembers what their BSM instructor has taught them about moving off uphill. In particular, check

that they understand how the clutch works and what happens as they manipulate the pedal. (See *Pass Your Driving Test*, pages 23–24.) Also check that the learner can remember the sequence to use when moving off uphill and what is different from moving off on a level road. (See *Pass Your Driving Test*, page 30 and pages 32–33.)

Major Points to Check During Practice

- Carries out Cockpit Drill correctly
- Completes safety checks before starting the engine
- Selects the correct gear

● *The learner will find they need more gas to move off when going uphill.*

- Sets sufficient gas
- Prepares the handbrake
- Holds the clutch at biting point
- Releases the handbrake while keeping feet still
- Keeps the car still while observations are carried out, including the blind spot
- Signals if necessary
- Moves away smoothly
- Steers to normal driving position
- Uses MSM routine to stop safely
- Parks accurately and smoothly facing uphill.

Advanced Exercises

(a) On a quiet road use a stopwatch to encourage reducing the time it takes to move away safely.

(b) Practise with the radio on so that the engine note cannot be heard.

(c) Practise on busier roads to develop judgement in selecting the first safe gap in the traffic.

(d) Practise on steeper hills.

(e) Practise at traffic lights on hills.

Common Problems

● Stalls

● Sets too little gas, or does not keep feet still when looking around

● Lets clutch up too quickly as the car moves

● Unable to find and hold biting point

● Comes off gas too early when stopping.

● *Practise starting and stopping on steeper hills.*

Session 5

Moving Off and Stopping Downhill

Where and When to Practise

Find a quiet, reasonably wide road with ideally a fairly long and gentle downhill slope and not too many parked cars. Park just after the start of the hill, facing down it.

Do not park just over the brow of a hill where you might cause danger to other traffic. Most learners have little difficulty moving off safely and smoothly downhill, but they do have a tendency to forget that the way to control the car is different.

General Safety

- Avoid any road where children are playing
- Personally check that it is safe before moving off
- Make sure you are a reasonable distance from any car parked ahead of you

● *Be prepared — the car may move off faster than expected.*

- Do not let the learner coast downhill
- The car may move off faster than expected; be prepared to prompt the learner to use the brake.

Explain What Is to Be Practised and How

Check Knowledge and Understanding

Ask a few questions to check that the learner remembers what their BSM instructor has taught them about moving off downhill. In particular, check that the learner understands the need to move away using the brake to

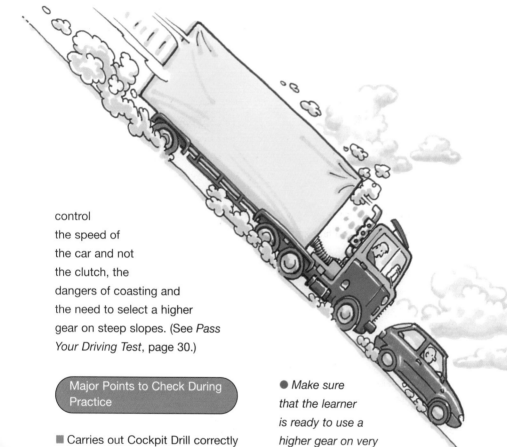

control
the speed of
the car and not
the clutch, the
dangers of coasting and
the need to select a higher
gear on steep slopes. (See *Pass Your Driving Test*, page 30.)

Major Points to Check During Practice

■ Carries out Cockpit Drill correctly
■ Completes safety checks before starting the engine
■ Selects the appropriate gear
■ Applies the footbrake firmly
■ Releases the handbrake
■ Makes adequate observations
■ Achieves smooth co-ordination releasing the footbrake, letting the

● *Make sure that the learner is ready to use a higher gear on very steep hills.*

clutch up smoothly and setting the gas, if needed

- Uses MSM to stop
- Uses the footbrake to adjust speed and park safely facing downhill
- Avoids coasting or riding the clutch.

Advanced Exercises

(a) Remain on a quiet road and use a stopwatch to encourage reducing the time it takes to move away safely.

(b) Practise on busier roads to develop judgement in selecting the first safe gap in the traffic.

(c) Practise on steeper hills where second gear would be appropriate.

(d) Practise at traffic lights on hills.

Common Problems

- Forgets the procedure
- Does not notice the car is facing downhill, causing the car to roll forward as the handbrake is released before checking it is safe to move off
- Keeps the clutch down too long and creates a jerky start
- Uses first gear on a very steep hill
- Does not brake hard enough on the downhill gradient to stop the car at the intended place.

- *Ensure the learner applies the footbrake firmly.*

Session 6

Changing Up to Second and Third Gear

Where and When to Practise

Ideally for the first few practices you need to find a quiet, long, straight, level road, which is reasonably wide and with not too many parked cars. Remember that unless the BSM instructor has already taught the learner how to turn left, you may need to stop before the end of the road, change seats, turn the car round and continue practising in the opposite direction.

General Safety

■ Avoid any road where children are playing
■ Personally check that it is safe before moving off
■ Make sure you are a reasonable distance from any car parked ahead of you

● *Be prepared for the car to veer to one side as the learner takes one hand off the wheel to change gear.*

- To start with, tell the learner when to change gear
- Do not ask the learner to change gear when too close to a parked car
- Be prepared for the car to steer to one side as the learner takes one hand off the wheel to hold the gear lever
- Make sure the car is travelling in a straight line when you ask the learner to change gear.

● *Check that the learner can select the gears without looking down.*

Explain What Is to Be Practised and How

Check Knowledge and Understanding

Ask a few questions to check that the learner can remember what their BSM instructor has taught them about changing gear. (See *Pass Your Driving Test*, pages 24–25.) With the engine off, check that they can select first, second and third gear using the clutch and gas correctly and without looking at the gear lever.

Major Points to Check During Practice

- Carries out Cockpit Drill correctly
- Completes safety checks before starting the engine
- Moves off safely and smoothly
- Uses mirrors effectively
- Places hand on gear lever appropriately without looking down
- Stays in control of steering
- Pushes the clutch right down and comes off the gas at the same time
- Selects the appropriate gear

● *A common problem is looking down at the gear lever and losing control.*

■ Lets the clutch back up with a little gas
■ Returns both hands to the steering wheel
■ Completes the gear change before the car slows down too much
■ Uses MSM to stop safely
■ Parks smoothly, without stalling the

engine while remaining in second or third gear.

Advanced Exercises

(a) Practise on a quiet road and allow the learner to decide when the speed is right to change gear.
(b) Practise changing gear when going uphill.
(c) Practise changing gear when going up a steep hill.
(d) Practise changing gear when going downhill.

Common Problems

● Looks down at the controls
● Steers off course as one hand comes off the wheel
● Selects the wrong gear
● Does not come off the gas as the clutch goes down
● Forgets to push the clutch down
● Takes too long to complete the gear change, so that the car is now travelling too slowly for the new gear.

Session 7

Turning Left from a Major to a Minor Road

Where and When to Practise

If possible, you need to choose a quiet series of level roads with good visibility where you can keep going round the block, turning and emerging to the left. If you start on a major road your first left turn will be into a minor road. The next time you turn left it will probably be into a major road. From the major road you can turn left again into a minor road and so forth until you are back where you started.

BSM recommends that you do not attempt this practice session until the learner has been taught by their BSM instructor both to turn left from major to minor roads and also to emerge left from minor to major.

General Safety

- All the safety rules and procedures concerned with moving off and stopping apply to all future practice sessions and will not be listed again
- Avoid practising where cars are parked too close to the junction where you wish to turn, whether before or after the turn
- This practice is not primarily concerned with emerging from minor roads, but you need to ensure it is safe when you do so
- Personally check it is safe each time before you turn left

● *Be prepared to take control of the wheel when absolutely necessary.*

- Always be ready to prompt the learner to steer or, when absolutely necessary, to take control of the wheel yourself
- If the speed is too fast on approach, prompt the learner to slow down before it is too late.

Explain What Is to Be Practised and How

When you first practise this exercise it is safest to be in second gear on approach to the turn.

Check Knowledge and Understanding

Ask a few questions to check that the learner can remember what their BSM instructor has taught them. In particular, that they understand the Mirror, Signal, Position, Speed, Look (MSPSL) sequence and how to use it. (See *Pass Your Driving Test*, pages 38–40 and 49.)

● *Learners sometimes forget to correct the steering after a turn.*

● *Make sure the learner does not swing out before turning.*

Advanced Exercises

(a) Practise on hills facing up and down.
(b) Practise where there are parked cars near the junction.
(c) Practise where there are pedestrians and other traffic.
(d) Practise at traffic lights.
(e) Practise all the above but approach in third or a higher gear and change down as appropriate.

Major Points to Check During Practice

■ Uses the mirrors effectively
■ Gives correct signal at an appropriate time
■ Takes up correct position before turning
■ Drives at an appropriate speed on approach
■ Observes before turning
■ Steers sufficiently and at correct time to turn
■ Does not swing out before or after turning
■ Straightens wheel at the correct time
■ Checks the mirrors after turning into the new road.

Common Problems

● Fails to check mirrors or checks mirrors and signals simultaneously
● Takes up incorrect position
● Maintains too fast a speed on approach
● Looks too late or insufficiently
● Steers too early and back wheel clips the kerb
● Steers too late and wide
● Does not correct the steering, or does so too late
● Makes no mirror check on major road
● Changes gear too late
● Does not let clutch fully up before steering.

Session 8

Emerging Left from a Minor to a Major Road

Where and When to Practise

If possible, you need to choose a quiet series of level roads with good visibility where you can keep going around the block, emerging and turning left, just as in Practice Session 7.

BSM recommends that you do not attempt this practice until the learner has been taught by their BSM instructor both to turn left from major to minor roads and also to emerge left from minor to major.

General Safety

■ Avoid practising where cars are parked too close to the junction where you wish to turn, whether before or after the turn

■ This practice is not concerned with turning left into minor roads, but you need to ensure it is safe when you do so

■ Personally check it is safe each time before you emerge

■ Be especially aware that the learner may find it difficult to judge the speed of other traffic and then select a safe gap

■ Always be ready to prompt the learner to steer or, when absolutely necessary, to take control of the wheel yourself

■ If the speed is too fast on approach, prompt the learner to slow down before it is too late.

● *Personally check it is safe each time before you emerge.*

● *Ensure the learner*
accelerates sufficiently
on the major road...

Explain What Is to Be
Practised and How

When you first practise
this exercise it is safest to be in
second gear on approach. To begin
with the learner is likely to stop and
select first gear before emerging, but
will gradually learn to slow down and
give way as appropriate.

Check Knowledge and
Understanding

Ask a few questions to check that the
learner can remember what their
BSM instructor has taught them
about emerging left from a minor to a
major road. In particular, check that
they understand the different road
priorities and the meaning of Give
Way and Stop signs and road
markings. Check that they
understand the sequence Mirror,
Signal, Position, Speed, Look
(MSPSL) and how to use it. (See *Pass
Your Driving Test*, pages 42–43.)

Major Points to Check During
Practice

■ Uses mirrors effectively
■ Gives correct signal at an
  appropriate time
■ Takes up correct position on approach
■ Adjusts speed appropriately on
  approach
■ Observes before/during emerging
■ Selects a safe gap
■ Steers sufficiently and at correct
  time to turn
■ Positions correctly in the major road
■ Checks the mirrors after turning into
  the new road
■ Accelerates sufficiently on the major
  road to avoid causing other vehicles
  to slow down.

Advanced Exercises

(a) Practise on hills facing up and
    down.

(b) Practise where there are parked cars near the junction.

(c) Practise where there are pedestrians and other traffic.

(d) Practise at closed junctions where you will need to stop.

(e) Practise where visibility is very restricted and you need to edge forwards to see better.

(f) Practise at open junctions where you may be able to slow down and emerge without stopping.

(g) Practise all the above but approach in third or a higher gear and change down as appropriate.

● *Learners may sometimes stop unnecessarily when it is clear that it is safe to keep moving.*

Common Problems

● Does not check mirrors or checks mirrors and signals simultaneously
● Takes up incorrect position
● Drives too fast on approach
● Looks too late or insufficiently
● Cannot judge a safe gap
● Stops unnecessarily when safe to keep moving
● Prepares and decides too slowly and misses gaps
● Steers too early and back wheel clips the kerb
● Straightens up too late after the turn
● Forgets the mirror check on major road
● Does not accelerate sufficiently on major road.

Session 9

Turning Right from a Major to a Minor Road

Where and When to Practise

If possible, you need to choose a quiet set of level roads with good visibility where you can keep going round the block turning right and emerging to the right, in a similar way to Practice Session 7.

BSM recommends that you do not attempt this practice until the learner has been taught by their BSM instructor both to turn right from major to minor roads and also to emerge right from minor to major.

General Safety

■ This practice is not primarily concerned with emerging to the right into major roads, but you need to ensure it is safe when you do so
■ Personally check it is safe each time before you turn left
■ Be especially aware that the learner may find it difficult to judge the

speed of oncoming traffic and select a safe gap
■ Always be ready to prompt the learner to steer or, when absolutely necessary, to take control of the wheel yourself
■ If the speed is too fast on approach, prompt the learner to slow down before it is too late.

● *Make sure the correct position is taken up before turning right.*

Explain What Is to Be Practised and How

When you first practise this exercise it is safest to be in second gear on approach. To begin with the learner will sometimes stop and give way to any oncoming traffic, even if there is a safe gap. They will gradually learn to slow down and turn or give way as appropriate.

● *The learner may not judge a safe gap.*

Check Knowledge and Understanding

Ask a few questions to check that the learner can remember what their BSM instructor has taught them about turning right from major to minor roads. In particular, check that they understand the sequence Mirror, Signal, Position, Speed, Look (MSPSL) and how to use it when turning right. (See *Pass Your Driving Test*, pages 40–41 and 48–49.)

Major Points to Check During Practice

■ Uses mirrors effectively
■ Gives correct signal at an appropriate time
■ Takes up correct position on approach
■ Drives at an appropriate speed on approach
■ Selects the correct gear
■ Observes adequately on approach
■ Times approach to select a safe gap or give way as necessary
■ Takes up correct position before turning
■ Makes a final check of right-hand mirror
■ Steers sufficiently and at correct time to turn
■ Positions correctly in the minor road
■ Checks the mirrors after turning into the new road.

Advanced Exercises

(a) Practise on hills facing up and down.
(b) Practise where there are no central road markings.
(c) Practise where there are pedestrians and busy traffic.
(d) Practise where there are queues of traffic.
(e) Practise at traffic lights.
(f) Practise all the above but approach in third or a higher gear and change down as appropriate.

● *Don't allow the learner to cut right-hand corners.*

Common Problems

● Does not check mirrors or checks mirrors and signals simultaneously
● Positions incorrectly or too late
● Drives too fast on approach
● Looks too late or insufficiently
● Cannot judge a safe gap
● Selects wrong gear or forgets to change gear
● Stops unnecessarily when safe to keep moving
● Unable to plan and time approach
● Takes too long to prepare and decide when to give way and misses gaps
● Steers too early and cuts the corner
● Forgets to check mirrors on minor road.

Session 10
Emerging Right From a Minor to a Major Road

Where and When to Practise

If possible, you need to choose a quiet set of level roads with good visibility where you can keep going round the block emerging and turning right, just as Practice Session 8 teaches emerging and turning left.

BSM recommends that you do not attempt this practice until the learners have been taught by their BSM instructor both to turn right and emerge right.

General Safety

■ Avoid practising where visibility is poor or where parked cars restrict vision or space

■ This practice is not primarily concerned with turning right into minor roads, but you need to ensure it is safe when you do so

■ Personally check it is safe each time before you emerge

■ Be especially aware that the learner may find it difficult to judge the speed of other traffic and select a safe gap

■ If the speed is too fast on approach, prompt the learner to slow down before it is too late.

● *Avoid practising where parked vehicles restrict the learner's vision or space.*

Explain What Is to Be Practised and How

When you first practise this exercise it is safest to be in second gear on approach. To begin with the learner is likely to stop and select first gear before emerging, but will gradually learn to slow down and give way as appropriate.

Check Knowledge and Understanding

Ask a few questions to check that the learner can remember what their BSM instructor has taught them about emerging right from minor to a major road and the particular dangers involved. In particular, check that they understand the different road priorities and the meaning of Give Way and Stop signs and road markings. Check that they understand the sequence Mirror, Signal, Position, Speed, Look (MSPSL) and how to use it. (See *Pass Your Driving Test*, pages 42–43 and 48–49.)

Major Points to Check During Practice

- Uses mirrors effectively
- Gives correct signal at an appropriate time
- Takes up correct position on approach
- Drives at an appropriate speed on approach
- Observes and makes safe decisions before and during emerging
- Stops or gives way when necessary
- Selects a safe gap
- Steers sufficiently and at correct time to turn
- Positions correctly in the major road
- Checks the mirrors after turning into the new road
- Accelerates sufficiently on the major road to avoid causing other vehicles to slow down.

Advanced Exercises

(a) Practise on hills facing up and down.

(b) Practise where there are parked cars near the junction.

(c) Practise where there are pedestrians and busy traffic.

(d) Practise at closed junctions where you will need to stop.

(e) Practise where visibility is very restricted and you need to edge forwards to see better.

(f) Practise at open junctions where you may be able to slow down and emerge without stopping.

● *Learners often stop too far back and cannot see into the new road.*

(g) Practise all the above but approach in third or a higher gear and change down as appropriate.

Common Problems

● Does not check mirrors or checks mirrors and signals simultaneously
● Takes up incorrect position
● Drives too fast on approach
● Looks too late or insufficiently
● Cannot judge a safe gap
● Stops too far back or forward
● Stops unnecessarily when safe to keep moving
● Prepares and decides too slowly and misses gaps
● Steers too early or late
● Forgets mirror check on major road
● Does not accelerate sufficiently on major road.

Session 11
Changing Up and Down Through All the Gears

Where and When to Practise

You need to find a road or series of roads that are reasonably straight and level without much traffic. One road with a speed limit over 30mph would be useful. BSM recommend that, as you will be travelling much faster, you do not attempt this practice unless you have already completed Practice Session 6 satisfactorily.

- Make sure the car is travelling in a straight line when you ask the learner to change gear
- Make sure it is safe behind, particularly before the learner slows down and changes down

General Safety

- To start with, you may need to prompt the learner when to change gear
- Do not ask the learner to change gear when too close to a parked car
- Be ready for the car to steer to one side as the learner takes a hand off the wheel to hold the gear lever. You practised this in Session 6, but the car will now be travelling much faster

● *To start with you may need to prompt the learner to change gear.*

- Take great care that first gear is not selected by mistake at high speed.

Explain What Is to Be Practised and How

You will be practising changing up and down through all the gears while

● *Make sure the learner keeps their eyes on the road ahead when practising gear changes while going downhill.*

travelling along a straight road. You are doing this to gain fluency and smoothness at gear changing and to get used to the speeds appropriate for each gear. You must not slow down and change down when other traffic is behind you on an open road, as they will not expect you to act like this. Remember this is simply practice and not how you would normally drive.

Check Knowledge and Understanding

Ask a few questions to check that the learner can remember what their BSM instructor has taught them about changing gear. (See *Pass Your Driving Test*, pages 24–26.) With the engine off, check that they can select each gear in sequence both up and down, without looking at the gear lever.

Major Points to Check During Practice

■ Checks the mirrors
■ Places hand on gear lever appropriately; does not look down
■ Keeps steering in control
■ Pushes the clutch right down and comes off the gas at the same time
■ Selects the appropriate gear for the speed
■ Lets the clutch back up with a little gas
■ Returns both hands to the steering wheel
■ Completes the gear change up before the car slows down too much
■ Brakes sufficiently before selecting the next gear down.

Advanced Exercises

(a) Remain on a quiet road and allow the learner to decide without any prompts when the speed is right to change gear both up and down.

(b) Practise changing gear up and down when going uphill.

(c) Practise changing gear up and down when going up a steep hill.

(d) Practise changing gear when going downhill.

(e) Practise block gear changing both up and down.

(f) Practise braking in the high gears and selecting first gear while the car is still moving slowly.

Common Problems

● Looks down at the controls
● Steers off course as one hand comes off the wheel
● Selects the wrong gear by mistake
● Selects the wrong gear for the speed and conditions
● Does not come off the gas as the clutch goes down
● Forgets to push the clutch down
● Takes too long to complete a gear change up so that the car is now travelling too slowly for the new gear selected
● Does not slow down enough before changing down.

● *Take great care that first gear is not selected at high speed.*

Session 12

Moving Off At an Angle

Where and When to Practise

Both the learner and the person accompanying them can feel nervous when practising this exercise due to the close proximity of the other vehicle. Before attempting this practice you may wish to imagine a parked car ahead and check the learner's confidence by carrying out the practice and moving out around the pretend car. Alternatively you could position a tall cone or other marker in a quiet road to represent the off-side rear of a parked car.

BSM recommend that you do not attempt this practice until the learner can move off fluently on a level road and is confident with clutch control. Their BSM instructor will, of course, advise when they are ready.

Before you start this session, find a quiet, level road which is reasonably wide with sufficient gaps between the parked cars to allow the learner to park about a car length behind the vehicle in front.

● *Look particularly for oncoming traffic the learner may not see.*

General Safety

- Avoid any road where children are playing
- Personally check that it is safe before moving off
- Keep looking all around as the car starts to move
- Look particularly for oncoming traffic into whose path the learner might pull out
- Be aware that the learner may not correct the steering quickly enough and finish positioned too wide or on the wrong side of the road
- Be sensitive to the owners/drivers of parked cars — your L-plates may make them apprehensive as they see the learner get closer and closer to their dream car.

Explain What Is to Be Practised and How

The objective is to move off safely and under control around the parked car in front, drive a short distance and park again on the left somewhere safe and suitable to try again.

Check Knowledge and Understanding

Ask a few questions to check that the learner can remember what their BSM instructor has taught them about moving off at an angle. Check in particular that they recognise the need to use the clutch to control speed and the need to allow time to steer; and check also that they are aware of the necessity for frequent observations all around. (See *Pass Your Driving Test*, pages 30 and 32–33.)

Major Points to Check During Practice

- Prepares the controls of the car to be ready to move — correct gear, adequate gas, clutch at biting point and handbrake
- Observes to check it is safe, including blind spot check
- Signals if necessary
- Achieves slow speed with clutch control
- Maintains smooth co-ordination as the car starts to move
- Steers briskly
- Corrects steering to achieve normal driving position
- Selects a safe place to stop
- Uses Mirror, Signal, Manoeuvre (MSM) when stopping
- Brakes gently to a stop
- Positions accurately when stopping by the kerb.

Advanced Exercises

(a) Remain on a quiet road, and gradually reduce the gap from the parked car in front.

(b) Practise on slightly busier roads, attempting to take advantage of the first safe gap in the traffic.

(c) Practise on an uphill gradient.

(d) Practise on a downhill gradient where brake control will be necessary.

Common Problems

● Stalls because of the need to steer more than usual

● Moves off too fast to steer sufficiently due to poor clutch control

● Steers too gently

● Jerks due to poor clutch control

● Observes inadequately, especially not looking several times as the car edges out

● Fails to notice oncoming traffic

● Corrects the steering too late and finishes up too wide.

● *Poor clutch control may make the learner move off too fast to control the steering.*

Session 13

Reversing Around a Corner to the Left

Where and When to Practise

Find a quiet junction where the roads are level, with no parked cars in the vicinity of the corner around which the learner will practise reversing. The corner should be reasonably sharp, nearly a right angle. You may find it useful to check that the learner can reverse slowly in a straight line, for a reasonable distance, before you attempt this practice. Their BSM instructor will have taught them both this and the left reverse, but the change to a different car can sometimes cause problems.

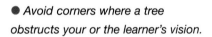

● *Avoid corners where a tree obstructs your or the learner's vision.*

■ Check particularly for oncoming traffic as the learner begins to steer because the front of the car will swing out.

General Safety

■ Avoid corners where a tree or post-box is near the kerb or obstructs vision
■ Avoid any road junctions where children are playing
■ Personally check that it is safe just before the car starts to reverse
■ Keep checking all around as the car starts to move

Explain What Is to Be Practised and How

Stop in the major road before the corner which the learner is going to reverse around. This allows them to assess the corner and then to drive past it and stop in a suitable position to start the practice.

● *The learner should reverse reasonably close to the kerb.*

Check Knowledge and Understanding

Ask a few questions to check that the learner can remember what their BSM instructor has taught them about reversing to the left. (See *Pass Your Driving Test*, pages 88–95 and 98–99.)

Major Points to Check During Practice

■ Positions safely and suitably in order to commence the reverse
■ Looks into turning for any problems
■ Prepares to reverse correctly, including seating position and grip on steering wheel
■ Looks all around before the car moves
■ Looks back over left shoulder whilst reversing in a straight line towards the corner with frequent glances to the front
■ Checks all round before steering and especially over right shoulder before the front of the car swings out
■ Keeps reasonably close to the kerb
■ Looks over left shoulder having

● *The learner should check all round before steering.*

rounded the corner with frequent glances to the front
- Uses clutch to control speed throughout the exercise unless going downhill
- Continues to reverse in a straight line for a reasonable distance and stops safely
- Gives way to other traffic or pedestrians as necessary.

Advanced Exercises

(a) Practise on corners which are long, gentle curves, not right angles.
(b) Practise reversing uphill around corners.
(c) Practise reversing downhill around corners.
(d) Practise around corners where the start road is level or slightly uphill as you reverse and changes to sharply downhill as you reverse into the new road.
(e) Practise on corners where there are no kerbstones to help judge the position.

Common Problems

- Observes inadequately and especially fails to check to the front and sides before steering
- Does not notice other vehicles and does not give way
- Reverses too fast and not in control
- Starts too close to the kerb, too near to the corner or not parallel to the kerb
- Steers too early or late
- Corrects steering too early or late to maintain position.

- *Make sure the learner is prepared to give way to pedestrians.*

Session 14

Reversing Around a Corner to the Right

Where and When to Practise

Find a quiet junction where the roads are level, with no parked cars in the vicinity of the corner around which the learner will practise reversing. The corner should be reasonably sharp, nearly a right angle.

BSM recommends that the learner does not attempt this practice until they can reverse to the left with confidence. Their BSM instructor will, of course, advise when they are ready.

oncoming traffic as the learner begins to steer since the front of the car will swing out
■ Remember that you are actually reversing on the wrong side of the road in the path of oncoming traffic. Frequent forward checks are needed. Once round the corner, always reverse back until you are

● *Reverse back until well clear of the junction.*

General Safety

■ Avoid corners where a tree or post-box is near the kerb or obstructs vision
■ Avoid any road where children are playing
■ Personally check that it is safe just before the car starts to reverse
■ Keep checking all around as the car starts to move
■ Check particularly for

● *Make sure the learner is still prepared to give way to pedestrians.*

well clear of the junction — about six car lengths.

Explain What Is to Be Practised and How

Stop on the left in the major road before the corner which the learner is going to reverse around. This allows them to assess the corner and, when safe, move off, cross to the right side of the road and park beyond the junction in a suitable position from which to reverse around it.

Check Knowledge and Understanding

Ask a few questions to check that the learner can remember what their BSM instructor has taught them about reversing to the right. (See *Pass Your Driving Test*, pages 96–99.)

Major Points to Check During Practice

■ Positions safely and suitably in order to commence the reverse
■ Looks into turning for any problems

■ Prepares to reverse correctly, including seating position and grip on steering wheel
■ Looks all around before the car moves
■ Looks over right shoulder when reversing to the corner with frequent glances to the front
■ Checks all round before steering
■ Keeps reasonably close to the kerb
■ Looks over right shoulder, having rounded the corner with frequent glances to the front
■ Uses clutch to control speed throughout the exercise unless going downhill
■ Continues to reverse in a straight line for a reasonable distance and stops safely well back from the junction
■ Gives way to other traffic or pedestrians as necessary.

Advanced Exercises

(a) Practise on corners which are long, gentle curves, not right angles.

(b) Practise reversing uphill around corners.

(c) Practise reversing downhill around corners.

(d) Practise around corners where the start road is level or slightly uphill as you reverse and changes to sharply downhill as you reverse into the new road.

(e) Practise on corners where there are no kerbstones to help judge the position.

Common Problems

● Observes inadequately, especially failing to check to the front often enough and before steering

● Does not notice other vehicles and not giving way

● Reverses too fast and not in control

● Starts too close to the kerb, too near to the corner or not parallel to the kerb

● Steers too early or too late

● Loses control when correcting the steering and fails to maintain position.

● *Check that it is safe before the learner begins to reverse, as they may not notice another vehicle.*

Session 15

Turning the Car in the Road

Where and When to Practise

Find a quiet and fairly wide, level road, preferably with a reasonably gentle camber. Park on the left, well away from parked cars on either side of the road and any trees or other obstacles close to the kerb.

General Safety

● *Don't scare pedestrians by driving or reversing towards them.*

- Avoid conducting this practice where a tree or post-box is near the kerb and would be immediately in front or behind as you drive across the road and reverse back
- Avoid any road where children are playing
- Personally check that it is safe throughout the manoeuvre
- Check particularly for other traffic, and when necessary advise the learner to give way
- Do not drive or reverse towards pedestrians on the pavement
- If other traffic waves at the learner to continue, be sure they really mean it
- Be aware that another car waiting puts pressure on the learner and may cause them to stall.

Explain What Is to Be Practised and How

The learner is going to turn the car around in the road by means of forward and reverse gears and then park on the left.

Check Knowledge and Understanding

Ask a few questions to check that the learner can remember what their BSM instructor has taught them about the turn in the road. (For a full account see *Pass Your Driving Test*, pages 100–107.)

Major Points to Check During Practice

■ Parks safely and suitably in order to commence the manoeuvre
■ Looks all around before the car moves
■ Waits for any traffic to pass
■ Looks in appropriate directions to check it is safe throughout the manoeuvre
■ Controls the speed
■ Steers briskly and steers back at the appropriate time
■ Applies the handbrake when stopped at the end of each phase of the manoeuvre
■ Maintains control and does not roll forwards or back on the camber
■ Avoids touching the kerb
■ Parks safely at the end of the manoeuvre.

● *Avoid touching the kerb.*

Advanced Exercises

(a) Practise on increasingly narrow roads.

(b) Practise on roads where some other traffic is likely to pass during the manoeuvre.

(c) Practise on hills facing up at the start of the manoeuvre.

(d) Practise on hills facing down at the start of the manoeuvre.

(e) Practise on roads with a steep camber.

Common Problems

● Observes inadequately, too long before the car moves, not looking in the direction the car is moving, or looking too long in one direction

● Fails to notice other vehicles and does not give way

● Does not notice pedestrians

● Drives forward or reverses too fast and not in control

● Fails to reverse the steering as the car nears the kerb

● Hits or mounts the kerb

● Does not switch from clutch control to brakes on a steep camber and loses control

● Takes excessive time to complete the manoeuvre and holds up the traffic.

● *Practise on a steep camber...*

Session 16
Reversing into a Parking Space

Where and When to Practise

Find a car park where at least one section is reasonably quiet and which has clearly marked parking bays. Initially you may find it less stressful to choose a bay for the learner to park in with another car on one side only and without another occupied bay or a brick wall immediately behind it.

● *Stop the practice and begin again if things start to go terribly wrong.*

General Safety

■ Keep a continuous lookout for other vehicles and pedestrians
■ Stop the practice and start again if things start to go terribly wrong
■ Do not allow the learner to get too close to any other vehicles.

Explain What Is to Be Practised and How

Stop in the car park somewhere safe, in a position where you can point out the bay into which you want the learner to reverse. In that way, they will be able to drive to a suitable position from which to reverse.

Check Knowledge and Understanding

Ask a few questions to check that the learner can remember what their BSM instructor has taught them about reverse-parking into a parking bay. In particular,

● *Make sure the learner does not protrude unnecessarily at the front.*

check that they understand the need for all-round continuous observation and the need to keep the car under control and moving slowly. (See *Pass Your Driving Test*, pages 114–115.)

Major Points to Check During Practice

■ Positions safely and suitably in order to commence the reverse
■ Prepares to reverse correctly, including seating position and grip on steering wheel
■ Looks all around before the car moves

■ Looks mainly over left shoulder when reversing, with frequent glances all around
■ Checks all round before steering and swinging to left or right
■ Reverses slowly under clutch control
■ Does not steer too much or too little
■ Stops within the parking bay
■ Stops parallel to the white lines and a reasonable distance from any car to either side
■ Stops before any obstruction to the rear of the vehicle
■ Does not protrude unnecessarily from the front of the parking bay.

Advanced Exercises

(a) Practise in a busier car park.

(b) Practise with an obstruction behind the parking bay and cars parked on both sides.

(c) Practise where limited space makes it difficult to find a position from which to reverse easily.

(d) Practise in a car park where the bays are narrower than normal.

(e) Practise reversing into a parking bay from the right.

Common Problems

● Attempts to reverse into the parking bay at right angles instead of drawing forwards at an angle and trying to reverse back as straight as possible

● Observes inadequately, especially failing to check all around before reversing and all the time the car is moving

● Looks out of the right-hand window to see the white lines at the expense of all-round observation

● Does not notice other vehicles or pedestrians and does not give way

● Reverses too fast and not in control

● Turns the steering wheel too much

● Parks outside the white lines

● Parks too far forward or back in the bay.

● *The learner may reverse too far back into the bay.*

Session 17 — Reverse Parking

Find a quiet, level road with a parked car which has a long gap behind it of at least three car lengths or no other car at all. Stop and park further back down the road in a position from which both you and the learner can see the gap into which you intend the learner to reverse.

General Safety

- Keep a continuous lookout for other vehicles and pedestrians
- Make sure you are not too near a bend or the brow of a hill
- Avoid roads where children are playing
- Do not choose a place that would block someone's driveway or narrow the road too much

- Be sure that it is legal to park there
- Avoid hills or steeply cambered roads for first attempts at this exercise
- Stop the practice and start again if things begin to go terribly wrong
- Do not allow the learner to get too close to any other vehicles.

● *Remember that car owners can become nervous if they see the learner getting too close to their pride and joy.*

Explain What Is to Be Practised and How

By stopping further back down the road, the learner has a chance to study the gap into which you wish them to reverse and to assess the situation. This will also allow the learner to drive off and stop safely, positioned in a suitable place from which to commence the reverse-park.

Check Knowledge and Understanding

Ask a few questions to check that the learner can remember what their BSM instructor has taught them about reverse parking. In particular, check that they understand the need for good all-round continuous observation and the need to keep the car under control and moving slowly. (See *Pass Your Driving Test*, pages 108–114.)

Major Points to Check During Practice

■ Warns other drivers of the intention, by giving an early signal if necessary
■ Positions safely and suitably in order to commence the reverse
■ Prepares to reverse correctly, including seating position and grip on steering wheel
■ Looks all around before the car moves
■ Looks mainly over left shoulder when reversing, with frequent glances all around
■ Checks all round before steering left, which brings the rear end of the car in, but swings the front end out into the road

● *Never try to reverse into a gap of less than one and a half times the length of your car.*

- Reverses slowly under clutch control
- Does not steer too much or too little
- Does not hit the kerb
- Stops parallel to the kerb and reasonably close to it.

Advanced Exercises

(a) Practise on busier roads

(b) Practise reversing into a smaller gap, but never less than one and a half car lengths.

(c) Practise on hills both up and down.

(d) Practise on a road with a very steep camber.

(e) Practise reversing into a gap on the right-hand side of the road. Either choose a very quiet road or a quiet one-way street.

Common Problems

- Stops too close to the car at the start of the exercise
- Observes inadequately before starting to reverse
- Makes no frequent checks ahead and all around
- Fails to look around before steering left
- Does not notice other vehicles or pedestrians and does not give way
- Going too fast and not in control
- Turns the steering wheel too much
- Straightens the wheels too late, the result being that the front of the car mounts the kerb
- Finishes up too far from the kerb.

Using Mirrors Effectively

Where and When to Practise

There is no specific when or where for this Practice Session. However, as far as possible select a route that covers only the types of situations and road conditions the learner has so far practised.

Each of the previous Recommended Practice Sessions (1–17) has involved using the mirrors effectively within the specific context of the topic being practised. This session starts to practise the general use of mirrors. All the sessions that follow require

● *Check that the learner understands the dangers of blind spots.*

considerable periods of general driving in a variety of road and traffic conditions. They focus on the particular topic to be practised during the session, but also provide an opportunity to spend a short period focusing on the effective use of mirrors during general driving. This is important in order to turn this essential skill into a habit.

General Safety

■ Always fit your own additional interior mirror so that you, as well as the driver, can see what is behind
■ Do not take it for granted that just because a learner looks in the mirrors, they will necessarily see and interpret what is happening
■ Never assume that a learner will act appropriately in relation to what has just been seen in the mirrors.

Explain What Is to Be Practised and How

The learner is going to go for a number of short drives practising the skills learnt so far, with the exception of the manoeuvres. The task is to focus on using the mirrors effectively, which means both looking at the right times and acting sensibly on what is seen.

● *Encourage the learner to use the door mirrors.*

Check Knowledge and Understanding

Ask a few questions to check that the learner can remember what their BSM instructor has taught them about the effective use of mirrors. Get them to explain why mirrors are important. Ask them to name as many situations as they can when they would need to use their mirrors. Ask them why using the door mirrors is important. Check that they still understand the dangers of blindspots. (See *Pass Your Driving Test*, pages 50–54 and page 29.)

Major Points to Check During Practice

Uses the mirrors before:
- Signalling
- Changing direction
- Turning or emerging left or right
- Overtaking or changing lanes
- Stopping or slowing down
- Increasing speed
- Approaching any hazard
- Opening car door.

Advanced Exercises

(a) Ask the learner to tell you every time they look in the mirrors.
(b) Ask them to say what they see every time they look in the mirrors.
(c) Ask the learner to tell you each time they look in the door mirrors.
(d) Ask the learner to say what they see in the mirrors and what action, if any, they need to take.

Common Problems

● Forgets to check the mirrors in any of the situations listed on the left
● Checks the mirrors too late
● Rarely uses the door mirrors
● Checks the mirrors at the same time as indicating
● Does not act sensibly on what is seen.

Session 19 — Giving Signals

Where and When to Practise

As with Session 18, there is no specific when or where for this Practice Session — although try to select a

● *Do not let the learner give confusing signals to other drivers.*

route that, as far as possible, covers only the types of situations and road conditions that the learner has so far practised.

Each of the previous Recommended Practice Sessions (1–18) has involved giving signals within the specific context of the topic being practised. This session starts to practise the

● *Do not let the learner wave to acquaintances across the street.*

general giving of signals. The sessions that follow all require considerable periods of general driving in a variety of road and traffic conditions; each session focuses on a particular topic to be practised and also provides an opportunity to concentrate for a short period on giving signals during general driving.

General Safety

■ Always fit your own additional interior mirror so both you and the learner can see what is behind

■ Many learners are confused by left and right; always check they have signalled the correct way

■ If the learner gives a confusing signal, ask them to cancel it

■ If a learner fails to signal, remind them to do so if it might cause problems for other road users

■ If a signal isn't cancelled, ask the learner to cancel it

■ Don't encourage the learner to wave pedestrians across the road, to use the horn as a rebuke or to use any signal not recommended by *The Highway Code*.

Explain What Is to Be Practised and How

A number of short drives to practise skills learnt so far, with the exception of the manoeuvres. The task is to focus on giving signals correctly, in good time and only when necessary.

Check Knowledge and Understanding

Ask a few questions to check the learner can remember what their BSM instructor has taught them about giving signals. Ask them to explain the purpose of signals and to give some examples of when they would need to signal. Can they give examples of unnecessary signals? And can they suggest situations where a signal might be confusing? (See *Pass Your Driving Test*, pages 55–59.) Can they demonstrate arm signals?

Major Points to Check During Practice

Signals are:
- Given when necessary
- Given in good time
- Cancelled at an appropriate time
- Not confusing.

Advanced Exercises

(a) Choose a road with two junctions fairly close together and ask the learner to turn down the second road; practise the timing of the signal so that it is not confusing.

(b) Ask the learner to park on the left just after a junction; practise the timing of the signal so that it is not confusing.

(c) Practise moving off in a road with a stream of traffic and deciding exactly when to signal.

Common Problems

- Signals to go round parked cars, which can be confusing particularly if there is a junction on the right
- Forgets to signal
- Signals in the wrong direction
- Forgets to cancel the signal
- Signals too early or too late.

● *Remind the learner to signal and not cause problems for other road users.*

Session 20
Dealing With Crossroads

Where and When to Practise

Find a reasonably quiet crossroads that has road markings indicating the major and minor roads. For the initial practices it is best to choose a place with good vision in all directions, without parked cars too near the junction and which is not staggered.

● *Crossroads can be dangerous places.*

General Safety

■ Crossroads can be dangerous places, so take extra care, particularly when turning right

■ Personally check it is safe before you turn or emerge

■ Be especially aware that the learner may find it difficult to judge the speed of other traffic and to select a safe gap

■ If the speed is too fast on approach, prompt the learner to slow down before it is too late.

Explain What Is to Be Practised and How

The learner will practise approaching the crossroads from all directions, turning left and right from the major to the minor road, emerging to the left and to the right from the minor to the major road, and going straight ahead.

Check Knowledge and Understanding

Ask a few questions to check the learner can remember what their BSM instructor has taught them about crossroads and the particular dangers involved. In particular, check that they understand the different road priorities at marked and unmarked crossroads and the meaning of Give Way and Stop signs and road markings. Check that they remember the sequence Mirror, Signal, Position, Speed, Look (MSPSL) and how to use it. Check also that they know when to position off-side to off-side and near-side to near-side when turning right with oncoming traffic also turning right. (See *Pass Your Driving Test*, pages 43–46 and 48–49.)

Major Points to Check During Practice

■ Uses the mirrors effectively
■ Signals correctly at an appropriate time
■ Takes up the correct position on approach
■ Drives at an appropriate speed on approach
■ Observes and makes decisions before and during turning or emerging
■ Stops or gives way when necessary
■ Selects a safe gap
■ Steers sufficiently and at correct time to turn
■ Positions correctly in the major road
■ Checks the mirrors after turning into the new road
■ Accelerates sufficiently on the major road to avoid causing other vehicles to slow down.

Advanced Exercises

(a) Practise on hills.
(b) Practise where there are parked cars near the crossroads.
(c) Practise where there is busy traffic.
(d) Practise turning right at staggered crossroads.
(e) Practise where there are traffic lights and box junctions.

● *Ensure the learner looks all around at a crossroads.*

Common Problems

● Does not check the mirrors or checks mirrors and signals simultaneously
● Takes up incorrect position
● Drives too fast on approach
● Looks too late or insufficiently
● Cannot judge a safe gap
● Stops too far back or forward
● Stops unnecessarily when safe to keep moving
● Prepares and makes decisions too slowly and misses gaps

● Steers too early or too late
● Fails to check mirrors on major road
● Accelerates insufficiently when on major road.

Session 21

Dealing With Roundabouts

Where and When to Practise

In order to practise this session efficiently it is best to try and find two or more roundabouts that are reasonably close together. You can then plan a series of routes that allow the learner to approach from different directions and exit to the left, right and straight ahead. You can also go all the way round the roundabout, double back on yourself and approach the previous roundabout from the opposite direction. Ideally, the roundabouts should have four entrances and exits, and two or more lanes approaching and leaving.

General Safety

■ Learners sometimes stop at a roundabout when the vehicle behind expects them to keep moving; keep a close look behind

■ When stopped behind another car at a roundabout, learners may keep

● *Learners may keep looking right and go without checking ahead.*

looking right, see a gap, and go without looking ahead; the car in front may not have moved, so beware

■ Personally check it is safe each time the learner joins a roundabout

■ The learner may misjudge the speed of traffic on the roundabout and not select a safe gap

■ If the speed is too fast on approach, prompt the learner to slow down before it is too late.

Explain What Is to Be Practised and How

The learner will practise approaching roundabouts and exiting to the left, right and straight ahead.

Check Knowledge and Understanding

Ask a few questions to check that the learner can remember what their BSM instructor has taught them about roundabouts, their purpose and the particular dangers involved. Check that they understand who has priority, how to approach, position and signal and how to use lane discipline for the different exits they will take. Check that they remember the sequence Mirror, Signal, Position, Speed, Look

(MSPSL) and how to use it. (See *Pass Your Driving Test*, pages 46–47.)

Major Points to Check During Practice

■ Uses MSPSL correctly on approach

■ Anticipates a safe gap and adjusts speed to keep moving when possible

■ Gives way when necessary

■ Selects the correct lane for the exit being taken

■ Signals correctly on approach, when on the roundabout and for the exit to be taken

■ Checks blindspot and signals before changing lanes

■ Keeps space from large vehicles, horse riders and bicycles.

Advanced Exercises

(a) Practise on busy roundabouts.

(b) Practise on roundabouts with more than four exits.

(c) Practise on roundabouts where the normal give-way rules are changed by the road markings.

(d) Practise on very large roundabouts which are one-way gyratory traffic systems and have many lanes, direction arrows on the lanes and many different direction signs and exits.

● *Keep space from large vehicles on roundabouts.*

(e) Practise on small roundabouts with only one lane at each entrance and exit.

(f) Practise on mini-roundabouts.

Common Problems

● Uses MSPSL too late on approach
● Positions in incorrect lane on approach
● Approaches at too fast a speed
● Hesitates or stops when safe to go
● When stopped, prepares and decides too slowly and misses gaps

● Signals incorrectly or too early or too late.
● Takes incorrect lane on roundabout for the exit chosen
● Does not stay in lane
● Does not look before changing lanes and cuts up other vehicles.

Session 22
Dealing With Pedestrian Crossings

Where and When to Practise

In order to practise this session efficiently, try and find a number of pedestrian crossings that are reasonably close together. You can then plan a series of routes that allow the learner to approach from different directions. You will need to provide the learner with experience of all the different types of pedestrian crossing, including those controlled by light signals.

■ If the learner approaches a crossing too fast and pedestrians are nearby, give an early warning to slow down

General Safety

■ Pedestrians are vulnerable and you need to take great care
■ Watch out particularly for pedestrians and children on the pavement, running in the direction of the crossing and with their backs to you; they may cross without looking
■ Try to personally spot each crossing as far ahead as possible so that you can judge if the learner is acting appropriately

● *Pedestrians and children are vulnerable, so watch out! They may cross without looking to see what's coming.*

■ Keep a careful watch for vehicles close behind who may not expect the learner to slow down or stop
■ Never wave pedestrians across the road or allow the learner to do so.

Explain What Is to Be Practised and How

The learner will practise approaching both controlled and uncontrolled crossings, spotting them well ahead, using MSPSL, giving way when appropriate and obeying light signals.

Check Knowledge and Understanding

Ask a few questions to check that the learner can remember what their BSM instructor has taught them about the different types of pedestrian crossing, how to deal with them and the dangers involved. Check that they understand the rules that govern different types of crossing and when, where and for whom they must stop by law or should stop to be safe and courteous. Check that they remember the sequence Mirror, Signal, Position, Speed, Look (MSPSL) and how to use it. Ask them to demonstrate a slowing-down arm signal and suggest when they might need to use it. (See *Pass Your Driving Test*, pages 120–127.)

● *The learner needs to use MSPSL early enough to be effective.*

Major Points to Check During Practice

■ Spots the crossing far enough ahead
■ Uses MSPSL early enough and correctly on approach
■ Anticipates actions of pedestrians and shows consideration
■ Slows down, gives way or stops when necessary
■ Anticipates traffic signals and obeys them
■ Gives slowing-down arm signal when needed
■ Checks it is safe before moving off
■ Makes progress and does not hold up other traffic unnecessarily.

● *Practice where there is a continual stream of pedestrians.*

Advanced Exercises

(a) Practise dealing with crossings that have a central island, both controlled and uncontrolled, staggered and straight.

(b) Practise where there are two lanes on approach to a crossing.

(c) Practise where there is a continual stream of pedestrians wanting to cross.

(d) Practise in the dark, when pedestrians are harder to see.

(e) Practise near schools at the beginning and end of the day to gain experience of school-crossing patrols.

Common Problems

● Spots the crossing too late

● Fails to anticipate actions of pedestrians, resulting in harsh, last-minute braking

● Uses MSPSL too late on approach

● Gives way unnecessarily

● Moves off without checking it is safe to do so

● Fails to anticipate light signals and brakes harshly to stop

● Remains stationary at an amber flashing light even if the crossing is clear.

Session 23
General Road Position and Lane Discipline

Where and When to Practise

Depending on where you live, you may be able to incorporate this Practice Session into some of the other sessions requiring the learner to drive to a particular place to carry out an exercise. The learner will already have practised normal positioning as part of earlier sessions when using MSPSL. You will need to plan a route or series of routes covering as many different types of road as possible, including one-way streets with two or more lanes, two-way roads with two lanes or more in each direction, narrow roads, roads with parked cars, and also country roads.

● *Take particular care with any road situations the learner hasn't practised in previously.*

General Safety

■ Don't allow the learner to remain in an incorrect position for any length of time; act immediately if in any danger

■ Bear in mind that on some roads the car may be travelling faster than in previous sessions

■ If necessary take a different route to that planned rather than let the learner switch lanes at the last minute.

Explain What Is to Be Practised and How

The learner will practise maintaining a safe position in relation to the kerb, parked cars and oncoming traffic whilst driving on a variety of roads. The learner will also practise lane discipline, driving in the centre of their lane, using the correct lane, changing lanes safely and selecting the correct lane or position when turning or emerging.

Check Knowledge and Understanding

Ask a few questions to check that the learner can remember what their BSM instructor has taught them about general road positioning and lane discipline. Ask them to describe the position they would take up or path they would follow in a variety of circumstances. Check that they understand lane procedure, how to use MSPSL

● *Get the learner to describe the position they would take up in a particular circumstance.*

to change lanes safely, and the different rules that apply to one-way streets.

Major Points to Check During Practice

- Avoids driving in the gutter or too close to the kerb
- Avoids driving too close to the centre of the road or straddling the centre lines
- Avoids weaving in and out between parked cars
- Keeps space from parked cars
- Obeys the 'keep left' rule
- Drives in the middle of their lane
- Uses MSPSL to change lanes safely
- Takes up correct position when

turning or emerging, including in narrow roads

■ Takes up correct lanes for their intended direction in one-way streets

■ Keeps to the left on bends.

Advanced Exercises

(a) Practise on a greater variety of roads with more traffic.

(b) Practise in the dark when the position can be harder to judge.

Common Problems

● Drives too close to the kerb
● Drives too close to parked vehicles
● Forgets they are in a one-way street and positions in the left-hand lane to turn right
● Drives to one side of a lane or over the lane markings
● Steers abruptly or looks inadequately when changing lanes
● Leaves lane changes too late.

● *Learners may position incorrectly when they are in a one-way street.*

Session 24

Care in the Use of Speed

Where and When to Practise

The learner will, of course, practise this topic every time they drive. You can focus on speed for a few minutes

● *Don't allow the learner to break the speed limit.*

during any of the Practice Sessions. However, speed is so important to safety that it is well worth focusing on it for a whole session as well. You need to plan a route or set of routes

that include as many different types of road and traffic conditions and speed limits as possible, in town, village and country. Consider also driving down the same road at different times of day. The area near a school, for example, will be very different at start and finish times to the rest of the day, so a safe speed will also be different.

General Safety

■ Do not allow the learner to drive at speeds above their current level of competence
■ Do not allow the learner to break the speed limit
■ Do not allow the learner to drive excessively slowly and hinder other traffic
■ Encourage the learner to make progress, keep pace with other traffic, and not to be over-hesitant at junctions.

Explain What Is to Be Practised and How

The learner will practise making progress while maintaining a safe speed within the speed limits when driving on a variety of roads and in different traffic conditions.

Check Knowledge and Understanding

Ask a few questions to check that the learner can remember what their BSM instructor has taught them about driving at a safe speed. Ask them to explain why both driving too fast or too slowly for the conditions can be dangerous and get them to give examples. Do they know the speed limits for different types of road?

Ask them to describe how they will avoid being too hesitant at junctions and missing safe gaps. (See *Pass Your Driving Test*, pages 64–69 and 74–77.)

Major Points to Check During Practice

■ Keeps near to the speed limit when safe
■ Avoids breaking the speed limit
■ Takes advantage of safe gaps at junctions
■ Keeps up with other traffic within the speed limit
■ Reduces speed when space or visibility decreases
■ Uses anticipation to maintain steady progress
■ Uses anticipation to reduce speed well before hazards.

● *Ask why driving too fast for the conditions can be dangerous...*

● *Ensure that the learner does not crawl along and hold up other traffic.*

Advanced Exercises

(a) Practise on a greater variety of roads with more traffic.
(b) Practise in the dark when the learner may find it harder to judge speed and when a slower speed may be appropriate.
(c) While practising, ask the learner to state the speed of your car without looking at the speedometer.
(d) When possible practise in bad weather conditions, such as when it is raining.

Common Problems

● Changes speed erratically
● Copies other traffic and drives too fast for the conditions or breaks the speed limit
● Drives too fast in side roads and near pedestrians and children
● Drives too fast on approach to junctions and other hazards
● Drives too slowly for the conditions and holds up other traffic
● Does not take advantage of safe gaps at junctions
● Pulls out of a junction into a safe gap, but so slowly that another vehicle has to slow down.

Session 25 — Keeping Space from Traffic

Where and When to Practise

The learner will, of course, practise this topic every time they drive. You can focus on keeping space for a few minutes during any of the Practice Sessions. However, just like speed, keeping space is so important to safety that it is well worth focusing on it for a whole session as well. You need to plan a route or set of routes that include as many different types of road and traffic conditions and speed limits as possible, in town, village and country.

● *Ensure the learner uses the two-second rule.*

General Safety

■ Do not allow the learner to drive at speeds above their current level of competence and control

■ Ensure the learner stays within the speed limit

■ Do not allow the learner to drive too close to the vehicle in front

■ Be personally aware of the space

behind and to both sides as well as in front; less space means less speed. If necessary, ask the learner to slow down before things get out of hand.

Explain What Is to Be Practised and How

The learner will practise keeping space from other vehicles and road users when driving on a variety of roads and in different traffic conditions. In particular, they will practise using the two-second rule to help them judge a safe gap from the vehicle in front.

Check Knowledge and Understanding

Ask a few questions to check that the learner can remember what their BSM instructor has taught them about keeping space. Ask them to give examples of how lack of space to the sides might require them to reduce speed or change position. Ask them to describe the two-second rule and how to use it. Check that they know stopping distances and the effect of rain, ice and snow.

Major Points to Check During Practice

Reduces speed when:
- space is reduced
- close to children or other pedestrians
- the road narrows or is narrowed by obstructions
- close to oncoming vehicles;

And that the learner:
- maintains a safety gap from the vehicle in front
- uses the two-second rule to check the gap
- leaves a suitably bigger gap in bad weather.

Advanced Exercises

(a) Practise on a greater variety of roads with more traffic.
(b) Practise in the dark when the learner may find it harder to judge space and speed and when a slower speed and a larger gap may be appropriate.
(c) While practising, ask the learner to state how far away they think they are from the vehicle in front and whether that is more or less than a safe gap.
(d) When possible practise in bad

weather conditions, such as when it is raining.

Common Problems

● Fails to slow down when space to either side is reduced
● Drives too fast near pedestrians and children

● Fails to anticipate reduced space ahead and drives too fast
● Drives too close to the car in front
● Does not adjust the gap in front to account for weather conditions.

● *Less space means less speed.*

Session 26

Meeting Other Traffic

Where and When to Practise

'Meeting other traffic' is the term used to describe a situation where the road is narrowed to less than the width of two vehicles and there is a vehicle approaching you from the opposite direction. Since you will both be using the same space this is a hazard. Try to find a series of narrow roads or, more likely, roads that are narrowed because cars are parked on both sides.

General Safety

■ Be personally aware of the space to both sides and behind as well as the space in front; less space means less speed. Ask the learner to slow down if necessary, before things get out of hand

■ Look ahead for gaps between parked cars, and be ready to point out a suitable place for the learner to pull in and give way. This is safer than finding that the learner needs to reverse because they have not made use of MSM or planned for oncoming vehicles

■ Do not assume that the oncoming vehicle will give way just because the parked cars or other obstructions are on their side of the road

■ Take particular care if there is a vehicle close behind.

Explain What Is to Be Practised and How

The learner will practise meeting other traffic in roads where either the learner or the oncoming vehicle will need to select a suitable gap to pull into and give way.

Check Knowledge and Understanding

Ask a few questions to check that the learner can remember what their BSM instructor has taught them about meeting other traffic. Ask them to explain how they will use MSM when meeting other traffic. Find out what they understand by anticipation and why they think it is important in this situation. Also ask what factors they will consider when deciding whether to

keep going or give way. (See *Pass Your Driving Test*, pages 82–87.)

Major Points to Check During Practice

- Reduces speed early when the road narrows or is narrowed by obstructions
- Looks well ahead for oncoming vehicles
- Reduces speed early enough to make a decision to go or give way
- Looks for gaps to pull into and give way
- Leaves enough room to pull out of the gap when safe
- Normally gives way when the obstruction is on the learner's side of the road
- Notices passing places on narrow country lanes
- Does not hesitate unduly.

Advanced Exercises

(a) Practise on hills both up and down.

(b) Practise in the dark when the learner may find it harder to judge space, distance and the speed and size of an oncoming vehicle.

(c) Practise on busier side roads

● *Check that the learner remembers what is meant by 'meeting other traffic'.*

● *Look well ahead for gaps between parked cars.*

where there may be a stream of traffic in both directions.

(d) When possible practise in bad weather conditions, such as when it is raining.

Common Problems

● Fails to observe developing situations sufficiently far ahead
● Does not use MSM or fails to use it early enough, causing late braking or a need to stop and reverse

● Hesitates, unable to decide whether to keep going
● Waves the oncoming driver on
● Pulls into a gap and stops too close to a parked car or obstruction in front.

Session 27
Dealing With Dual Carriageways

Where and When to Practise

It is safest to start by finding a dual carriageway, not too busy and with two lanes in either direction. Initially, choose a place to join where there is an acceleration lane and a place to leave where there is a deceleration lane. This makes it much easier for the learner to practise joining and leaving.

● *End the practice when it is safe if the learner has difficulty staying in lane.*

General Safety

■ The learner may have had very limited practice to date at travelling at speeds of up to 70mph; you need to be even more vigilant than usual

■ If the learner finds difficulty staying in lane, end the practice as soon as it is safe; this may be due to the change from the BSM car to yours

■ Make frequent checks in your extra mirror, especially before asking the learner to change lanes, turn left or right or overtake

- Personally check the blindspot before changing lanes
- Do not allow the learner to drive too close to the vehicle in front
- Only overtake when there is ample time and space until the learner has practised 'Overtaking' in Session 28, next.

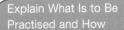
Explain What Is to Be Practised and How

The learner will practise joining, leaving and driving on dual carriageways, keeping pace with the traffic at up to the speed limit, looking well ahead, keeping space, lane discipline and simple overtaking.

Check Knowledge and Understanding

Ask a few questions to check that the learner can remember what their BSM instructor has taught them about driving on dual carriageways. Make sure they understand what they should do to join and leave, can use the two-second rule, and know how to use MSM to change lanes. (See *Pass Your Driving Test*, pages 70–72.)

● *Make sure the learner complies with lane discipline.*

Major Points to Check During Practice

- Uses any acceleration or deceleration lane appropriately to join or leave
- Joins and leaves safely where there is no acceleration or deceleration lane
- Drives in the centre of the lane
- Complies with lane discipline
- Keeps adequate space all around and especially in front
- Uses MSM to change lanes
- Changes lanes smoothly
- Turns right safely, including taking up the correct position

- Overtakes safely if required
- Does not drive too slowly and hold up the traffic, nor break the speed limit.

Advanced Exercises

(a) Practise joining and leaving where there are no acceleration or deceleration lanes.

(b) Practise turning right onto a dual carriageway where there is a wide, central reservation.

(c) Practise turning right onto a dual carriageway where there is a narrow central reservation.

(d) Practise in the dark and in bad weather.

Common Problems

- Builds up speed too slowly on the acceleration lane
- Does not observe developing situations sufficiently far ahead
- Fails to use MSM, or does not use it early enough
- Does not drive in the centre of the lane
- Steers too harshly when changing lanes
- Drives too close to the vehicle in front
- Drives too slowly
- Brakes in left-hand lane, when turning left, rather than waiting and using the deceleration lane to slow down.

● *Practise joining or leaving where there are no acceleration or deceleration lanes.*

Session 28 — Overtaking

Session 28

Where and When to Practise

Overtaking another moving vehicle is potentially the most dangerous driving situation, particularly on single carriageway roads. It is safest to start by finding a dual carriageway with two lanes in either direction, which is not too busy. This allows the learner to practise the routine of overtaking without the extra worry of oncoming traffic. Once the learner is confident you can move on to practise on two-way roads.

General Safety

■ Overtaking is a potentially dangerous manoeuvre, so exercise great care
■ You should always make your own decision as to whether it is safe to overtake; if in doubt, tell the learner to hold back
■ Remember that a learner may not always accelerate sufficiently to take advantage of a relatively short gap
■ Don't let the learner get too close to a vehicle before overtaking
■ Ensure the learner does not cut in too soon after overtaking
■ Watch out for harsh steering.

● *Watch out for harsh steering.*

Explain What Is to Be Practised and How

The learner will practise overtaking firstly on a dual carriageway and then on two-way roads.

Check Knowledge and Understanding

Ask a few questions to check that the learner can remember what their BSM instructor has taught them about overtaking. In particular, make sure they can explain when and why they would overtake, when and where not to overtake and how to use the

sequence MSPSL to overtake safely. It may be best to ask them to describe this sequence in some detail. Check also that they are aware of the problems cyclists can have when being overtaken. (See *Pass Your Driving Test*, pages 78–82 and 85–86.)

Major Points to Check During Practice

- Only overtakes when it is safe, legal and necessary
- Does not break the speed limit to overtake
- Positions correctly before overtaking
- Adjusts speed correctly
  - Judges speed of oncoming traffic
  - Judges the speed of vehicles behind
  - Signals at the correct time and cancels it as necessary
  - Chooses safe gaps in the traffic in which to overtake
  - Controls the car smoothly
  - Returns to the left safely after overtaking.

● *The learner may need help to judge a safe gap.*

● *The learner will need to practise overtaking long vehicles.*

Advanced Exercises

(a) Practise overtaking long vehicles.
(b) Practise overtaking a line of vehicles.
(c) Practise starting to overtake a line of vehicles and moving back safely into a gap on the left to allow a faster vehicle behind to go through.
(d) Practise overtaking when going up and down hill.
(e) Practise on a three-lane, two-way road.
(f) Practise in the dark and in the rain.

Common Problems

● Shows poor observation
● Demonstrates poor judgement of the speed of other vehicles
● Unable to judge own speed in relation to the vehicle to be overtaken
● Cannot judge the time and distance it will take to overtake
● Drives too close to the vehicle in front before overtaking
● Steers harshly
● Drives too close to the vehicle being overtaken
● Cuts in too soon after overtaking
● Forgets to return to the left lane after overtaking on a dual carriageway
● Returns to the left lane unnecessarily each time when overtaking a line of vehicles
● Drives too close when overtaking cyclists.

Session 29 — Assessing Risks

Where and When to Practise

In the early stages of learning to drive, the learner tends to concentrate largely on co-ordinating the controls at the expense of assessing what is going on around them. As confidence with the controls grows, more thought and energy can be concentrated on looking for risks, anticipating them and acting early to avoid problems. This skill takes time to develop and you can help the learner practise it in many of the preceding sessions.

In this session you will help the learner identify risks, make decisions and then act on them. You need to plan a series of varied routes which will pose different road and traffic conditions and involve pedestrians, children and cyclists. The first few routes should not take more than 15 minutes or so to drive around.

General Safety

■ Initially the learner may find it difficult to concentrate for more than a few minutes at a time; if a break is needed, stop

■ The learner may spot an actual risk — may even decide what to do about it — but then not act on the decision

● *The learner may find it difficult to concentrate for more than a few minutes at a time.*

● *Lack of past experience of similar situations means that the learner may not perceive a situation as a risk.*

■ The learner may not spot risks early enough
■ The learner needs to anticipate what may happen next, but lack of past experience of similar situations may make this difficult and means they may not perceive a situation as a potential risk.

Explain What Is to Be Practised and How

The learner will practise driving in varied conditions, assessing risks and potential risks, deciding what action to

take and then carrying out that action safely. The learner will gradually attempt to look for possible risks as far ahead as they can; they will also show by the way they constantly move their eyes that they are spotting problems all around, including behind.

Check Knowledge and Understanding

Ask a few questions to check the learner can remember what their BSM instructor has taught them about assessing risks. Discuss the need for total concentration and avoiding distractions. They will understand the task far easier if they have read *Pass Your Driving Test*, pages 130–135 and pages 142–151.

Major Points to Check During Practice

■ Looks well ahead
■ Moves their eyes all the time to look into the far, middle and near distance, into the mirrors and, where necessary, the blindspot
■ Spots problems and anticipates potential dangers
■ Decides what to do
■ Acts safely, by slowing down and keeping space, for example
■ Makes other road users aware of their intentions.

Advanced Exercises

(a) Practise for longer periods of time as concentration improves.
(b) Ask the learner to say the moment they see a risk.
(c) Get the learner to point out a risk and to suggest what might happen next.
(d) Ask the learner to say what risk they perceive and what action they are taking.

Common Problems

● Gets distracted whilst driving
● Loses concentration
● Focuses too much attention on one problem
● Fails to anticipate what might happen next
● Can't see any risk
● Can't decide what to do
● Is too late spotting a risk or acting on it.

● *The learner may not be able to decide what to do.*

Session 30

Commentary Driving

This Practice Session has two elements. In the first, you will drive and the learner will give a commentary from the passenger seat. In the second, the learner will both drive and give a commentary. This will help you establish exactly what the learner is looking at and what they see as important when driving, and will enable you to focus further practice on the risky situations that you feel the learner is failing to take into account.

To start with you need to plan short routes, which take perhaps five or ten minutes to drive around and which have varied road and traffic conditions. You may find it beneficial to repeat the same route several times.

General Safety

■ When you are driving, do not allow yourself to become over-distracted by the learner's commentary

■ When the learner is driving and giving a commentary their driving

● *You may find it beneficial to repeat the same route several times.*

may suffer initially from the extra mental effort needed

■ Start by simply asking the learner to point out risks they can see; gradually build on this so that they also predict potential problems and finally include what action they are taking

■ Avoid attempting this exercise for more than a few minutes at a time in the early stages.

Explain What Is to Be Practised and How

Firstly you will drive and the learner will point out all the risks they perceive to

be a problem. Then the learner will practise driving for short periods, in varied conditions, stating the risks they see as important and detailing what action they are taking to deal with them safely. Regardless of who is driving, the amount of detail that you ask the learner to give as a commentary should be built up gradually.

Check Knowledge and Understanding

Ask a few questions to check the learner can remember what their BSM instructor has taught them about developing commentary driving. Discuss the need for total concentration and avoiding distractions. They will understand the task far easier if they have read *Pass Your Driving Test*, pages 130–135 and pages 142–151.

● *Ask the learner to predict potential problems.*

● *The learner may become distracted from driving by giving a commentary.*

Major Points to Check During Practice

■ Looks well ahead for possible problems

■ Selects appropriate problems on which to comment

■ Proposes actions which are safe, well-timed and appropriate

■ Maintains a high level of concentration

■ Demonstrates all-round awareness through their commentary

■ Maintains control of the car to a reasonably high standard.

Advanced Exercises

(a) Practise for longer periods of time as concentration improves.

(b) Increase the amount of detail in the commentary.

(c) Practise on country roads.

(d) Practise in the dark.

Common Problems

● Distracted by giving a commentary at the same time as driving

● Initially embarrassed at speaking out loud

● Lacks concentration

● Focuses too much attention on one problem

● Has difficulty anticipating what might happen next

● Can't see any risk

● Can't decide what to do

● Spots a risk too late or takes too long to act.

Session 31 — Night Driving

Where and When to Practise

This Practice Session is divided into two tasks. The first involves practising driving at dusk and at night, in built-up areas and on other roads where there are street lights. Try to plan a route that involves a variety of well-lit main roads and more poorly lit back streets.

● *Avoid dazzling other drivers.*

The second task requires the learner to practise driving on unlit roads. You will need to plan a suitable route to include major two-way roads, dual carriageways and narrower country lanes. At least one practice for each element should start just before dusk, so that the learner can decide when to turn on the headlights and become familiar with the difficulty of seeing other vehicles that have no lights switched on.

General Safety

- Remind the learner to turn on the headlights if they fail to do so when necessary
- Do not allow the learner to dazzle other drivers
- Be ready to steady the wheel if the learner is dazzled by oncoming traffic
- Pay particular attention to speed, especially when passing oncoming traffic and approaching bends
- Watch out for cyclists and pedestrians who may be hidden in the gloom
- Take care at junctions where the speed of other traffic may be hard to judge.

● *Watch out for cyclists in the gloom.*

Explain What Is to Be Practised and How

The learner will practise turning on the headlights at the appropriate time, and then using dipped and full-beam lights, dipping headlights correctly and judging speed, space and visibility in the dark.

Check Knowledge and Understanding

Ask a few questions to check that the learner can remember what their BSM instructor has taught them about the extra dangers of driving in the dark. In particular, check that they can operate the light controls easily and know when and how to dip their headlights and return to full beam. (See *Pass Your Driving Test*, pages 152–155.)

Major Points to Check During Practice

- ■ Switches on dipped headlights when required
- ■ Uses full beam headlights on unlit roads when safe to do so
- ■ Avoids dazzling other road users and dips the lights when necessary and at the right moment
- ■ Adjusts speed to match conditions and visibility
- ■ Judges the speed of other traffic accurately
- ■ Judges space and distance accurately
- ■ Takes appropriate action when dazzled by another vehicle.

Advanced Exercises

(a) Practise at busy, complex junctions and roundabouts.

(b) Practise joining and crossing dual carriageways with a reasonable flow of traffic.

(c) Practise on unlit roads where there are a series of hills and bends.

(d) Practise on country roads where there are no cats' eyes.

(e) Practise reversing in the dark on both lit and unlit roads.

(f) Practise on a narrow country lane with passing places.

(g) Practise overtaking on unlit roads.

Common Problems

- ● Fails to notice that it is getting dark
- ● Forgets to dip headlights when needed
- ● Dips headlights too late
- ● Misjudges the speed of oncoming traffic.

● *The learner can become disorientated, especially when dazzled by oncoming headlights.*

Session 32

Driving in Bad Weather

Where and When to Practise

Practising with learners in bad weather, except in the rain, can be highly dangerous. BSM strongly recommends that you should not accompany a learner to drive in adverse weather conditions, other than rain.

In poor weather conditions, learners should only be accompanied by a BSM instructor in a dual-controlled car. Even then, the conditions may be too dangerous to allow tuition to continue. This Practice Session should not be conducted until the learner has passed the Practical Driving Test and has gained some experience as a newly-qualified driver in good weather conditions.

In the interests of safety, BSM further recommends that, whenever possible, newly-qualified drivers should undertake a practical lesson with a BSM instructor in each bad-weather scenario, before undertaking practice with an accompanying driver.

Planning a Practice Session

The weather forecast may allow you to plan a bad-weather practice session. You may equally need to seize the

● *Do not practise in snow, ice or fog until the learner has passed the Practical Test.*

opportunity when it arises. In the case of rain and fog, you should plan a route that includes a variety of different types of road both in and out of town. In snow and ice, it is safest to practise car control skills in a large car park or very quiet side roads before driving in traffic.

General Safety

■ Safety implications are clearly paramount in any practice in bad weather
■ Do not attempt to practise in extreme conditions or when organisations like the RAC advise you only to drive if your journey is essential
■ Ensure that your car is adequately prepared for the journey

■ Carry safety equipment, if appropriate.

Explain What Is to Be Practised and How

The newly-qualified driver will practise driving in one or more of the poor weather scenarios described above. They will practise preparing the car for the journey, using headlights, fog lights, wipers and demisters appropriately, keeping control and maintaining a safe speed.

● *The newly-qualified driver should make gentle use of the controls.*

Check Knowledge and Understanding

Ask a few questions to check the newly-qualified driver can remember what their BSM instructor has taught them about the extra dangers of driving in the specific bad weather conditions they are about to practise. Check in particular that they understand the relationship between a safe speed and visibility and the extra distance it takes to stop in rain, snow and ice. Check also that they understand how to avoid skidding and the principles of skid correction. (See *Pass Your Driving Test*, pages 64–69.)

Major Points to Check During Practice

The newly-qualified driver:
- checks and prepares the car for the journey
- uses lights correctly and turns them off when no longer needed
- uses windscreen wipers, washer and demisters as needed
- drives at an appropriate speed and keeps a safe distance from the vehicle in front
- makes gentle use of the controls and uses appropriate gears for the conditions.

Advanced Exercises

(a) Advanced exercises, except in the rain, are too dangerous to practise on a public road.
(b) Practise driving in the rain on dual carriageways where spray from large vehicles causes problems.
(c) Practise driving in the rain at night.

Common Problems

- Drives too fast for the weather conditions
- Drives too close to the vehicle in front
- Uses too low a gear in snow and causes wheelspin
- Forgets to use lights, wipers, windscreen washers, demisters, etc
- Does not check the car before making the journey
- Does not clear the windscreen of snow or ice adequately before moving off
- Leaves fog lights on when visibility improves.

Practice Sessions
A guide to accompanying the learner driver

Part
4

The Driving Test and Beyond

The Day of the Theory Test

Before the Test

Few people leap up and down with joy at the prospect of taking an examination of any sort, even though they may well do so at the moment they hear they have passed. A few test nerves are perfectly normal — indeed a bit of adrenaline pumping round the system can enhance concentration. Too much, and the mind tends to overheat, confusion takes over and what has been learnt becomes hard to recall. The Theory Test is no different to any other examination in this respect, and as with all such occasions, there are a number of things that people can do to help remain calm and in control.

Being well prepared is essential. The learner will achieve this if they have studied at home using suitable learning materials and taken full advantage of the facilities that BSM Centres have to offer. You can encourage them in both these respects.

Knowing what to expect helps reduce fear of the unknown.

The BSM touch-screen computers and question banks should have greatly helped in this respect. Once again, urge them to come into the Centre and use the equipment.

Arriving in plenty of time is far better than being in a rush. Time is needed to get used to the surroundings and complete the formalities. If they arrive after the test session has started they will not be allowed to sit the test.

Help the learner to avoid last-minute panics by ensuring that they have their appointment letter and have got the date and time correct. Also check that

● *Being well-prepared is essential.*

they have an appropriate form of photographic identification, such as both parts of their signed photocard licence, their passport or some other acceptable form of identification. The local BSM Centre can advise on other forms of acceptable identification. If nothing acceptable is available, a photograph of the learner together with a certifying statement from the

● *Arrive at the Test Centre in plenty of time...*

learner's BSM Approved Driving Instructor (ADI) — both signed by that ADI — is acceptable. For obvious reasons, do not leave it until the last minute to obtain suitable proof of identity.

During the Test

The learner is now on their own and beyond your help. You could remind them to:

- Use the practice questions they will be offered at the start of the test to ensure they are familiar with selecting and recording their answers using the touch-screen. These questions do not count towards the actual test mark
- Read each question very carefully before selecting an answer
- Avoid rushing, since they have plenty of time
- Flag up any questions they are not sure of and return to them before the end
- Use any time left to re-check, but to think carefully before amending any answers; if in doubt, leave the original answer unchanged
- Answer every question; it is better to guess than to leave a question blank
- Remember that at the end of the test they may be asked some trial questions for future question banks; these are not part of the test and neither these nor any customer survey questions asked will be used in determining their test score.

After the Test

The result should be available within 30 minutes at the Test Centre. If the candidate has followed the advice given by BSM their result is extremely likely to be a first-time pass. In the unlikely event of failure, urge them not to feel too disheartened and certainly not to give up. And remember that it can be of great help if you are able to bring them to the BSM Centre to discuss what went wrong and how to achieve a pass next time around.

● *During the test, the learner is on their own and beyond your control.*

The Day of the Practical Test

Before the Test

The day has finally arrived and both you and the learner are probably feeling a little nervous. If you have taken the advice of your BSM instructor, you can at least be sure that the learner is well prepared and stands a good chance of success.

Where possible you can help the learner in any of the following ways.

Make sure the learner gets a good night's sleep the night before the test and eats a good breakfast in the morning.

If for any reason the learner does not intend to take the test in a BSM car, it is essential that you ensure the test vehicle meets the requirements. It must display L-plates, be fitted with an extra internal mirror for use by the examiner and be in good roadworthy condition. The learner must bring the car's insurance certificate to the test. And you will need to accompany the learner to the Test Centre.

In a BSM car all this is taken care of and, of course, the BSM instructor will attend the Test Centre with the learner.

● *The BSM instructor will know more about the Test Centre's facilities than you may do.*

Learners normally have at least an hour's lesson with their BSM instructor immediately prior to the time of the test. This allows the instructor to calm the learner's nerves, boost their confidence and allow them to warm up and feel comfortable in the car. The instructor will ensure that they arrive in good time, and will also know whether that particular Test Centre has a toilet.

The learner must bring their provisional driving licence and some

● *The learner is now well and truly on their own...*

other acceptable proof of identity that bears their name, photograph and signature, as they had to for their Theory Test.

During the Test

The learner is now beyond your help, or that of the instructor, and everything rests on their safe demonstration of their driving skills.

The examiner will appear, call out their name and ask them to sign against it on a form. The examiner will also ask them to show proof of identity. The examiner will then ask which car is theirs and ask them to read a car numberplate from at least the required minimum distance. If they have forgotten their glasses they have a problem and if, after the examiner has measured the exact minimum distance to a numberplate, they still cannot read it, the practical drive will not take place and they will fail.

At the End of the Test

■ The examiner will tell the candidate whether they passed or failed
■ If they pass, the examiner will ask for their driving licence and give them a pass certificate
■ Make sure they send this certificate to DVLA Swansea when they apply for their full licence
■ The examiner will also give them a copy of the driving test report. This shows any faults that have been marked during the test so that the new driver is aware of their weaknesses and can make a conscious effort to improve
■ If they fail, the examiner will give them a Statement of Failure, which will include a copy of the driving test report. This will show all the faults that the examiner has marked during the test. The examiner will also spend a few moments explaining why they failed.

● *The examiner will tell the candidate whether they passed or failed.*

● *Never let anyone drive away from the Test Centre.*

After the Test

Whether they have passed or failed, encourage the learner to discuss the test report with their BSM instructor who will then be able to interpret it and explain what went wrong. The BSM instructor will also be able to advise the learner what action is needed if they have failed.

Regardless of the result, never let anyone who has just taken a test drive away from the Test Centre; their concentration will not be at its best, so drive for them.

Additional Driving Courses 1
Motorways

● *The first drive on a motorway can be a frightening experience.*

Learner drivers are not allowed to drive on motorways, nor is motorway driving part of the driving test. BSM has campaigned for many years to get this changed, as indeed have most organisations concerned with road safety. The Driving Standards Agency does, however, recommend that all new drivers seek professional help from an Approved Driving Instructor before driving on a motorway.

After passing the test, a new driver's first venture down a motorway can be very frightening. The motorway may be busy, the driver may well have forgotten some of the rules they learnt for the Theory Test, and they may find the speed of the other traffic alarming. It is not unusual to feel moments of sheer panic and fear.

BSM strongly recommends that you urge the learner you have been accompanying either to take up the two-hour BSM Motorway Simulator Course or to have a motorway lesson with a BSM instructor. Ideally they should do both.

BSM do not advise you to accompany a new driver on a motorway unless they have received some form of professional tuition. In a car with no dual controls, you are virtually powerless to take control should anything suddenly go wrong.

In-Car Motorway Lesson with a BSM Driving Instructor

The topics that a BSM instructor will teach and assess when giving a motorway lesson are also shown in the Learner Track Record which assesses whether the newly-qualified driver can:

- use relevant controls
- keep attention 1/2 mile ahead
- spot problems
- use signals
- time moves
- recognise signs and markings
- join the motorway

- drive at higher speeds
- judge the speed of other traffic
- judge the distance of other traffic
- follow at a safe distance
- drive in lanes
- change lanes
- overtake other traffic
- cope with roadworks
- leave the motorway

Motorway Simulator Course

The enormous advantage of the simulator is that all the basic motorway driving skills can be practised in complete safety. In addition, common problems are programmed to occur in exercises that, for safety reasons, could not be set up on a public road. Not only is this short course educationally valuable, it is also exciting and enjoyable.

As a learner works through a series of realistic exercises for about two hours, they:

- Learn how to use the simulator (for those new to it)
- Listen and watch as the simulator explains each topic using animated computer graphics to demonstrate what is required and the problems that need to be avoided
- Practise as the simulator monitors exactly how they are driving,

● *The simulator allows for situations that would be dangerous to create on a real motorway.*

including such items as position, speed, space from other vehicles and use of controls.

Practical exercises cover the following skills:

■ Joining — learning how to use the slip roads to join the motorway
■ Driving safely at speed and steering control
■ Changing lanes and using the correct lane
■ Keeping distance — keeping a safe distance from the vehicle in front
■ Overtaking — overtaking other vehicles safely
■ Keeping space — space to the sides and behind, as well as in front
■ Leaving — learning how to exit from a motorway.

At the end of each section of the course the simulator assesses progress and offers further in-depth practice of specific skills where needed:

■ The Final Drive — putting into practice all that has been learnt, as well as driving in rain, in fog, at night and through roadworks.

● *On the simulator learn how to use slip roads to join a motorway.*

Additional Driving Courses 2
Pass Plus, Risk Awareness, Night Driving

> Did you know that 85% of all accidents involve some form of human error?

Scary, isn't it? But don't worry, BSM would like to offer learner drivers better protection before they take to the road.

At BSM there are courses available to help the learner and the newly-qualified driver to improve their risk awareness when driving and reduce the chances of their becoming involved in an accident at all.

Pass Plus

The government has introduced a scheme for newly-qualified motorists called Pass Plus. It consists of six hours of training with a BSM instructor and covers such skills as town, night and bad-weather driving. Completion of this course not only

● *Pass Plus will improve different skills, such as bad-weather driving.*

● *The BSM instructor will point out where most everyday accidents occur.*

daily risks, by focusing on high-speed roads and built-up areas, which is where most accidents happen.

However, the course will be tailored to suit the particular area where the newly-qualified motorist lives, taking in motorway conditions wherever practical.

The BSM instructor will assess where the learner is putting themselves most at risk and will point out how and where the majority of everyday accidents occur. After discussing the likely risk areas, the instructor will suggest ways in which the driver can reduce those risks. They will then be able to practise what they have learnt.

prepares learners even further for safe driving, but they may be entitled to reduced insurance premiums with some insurance companies. Check out BSM Insurance Services.

BSM Risk Awareness Course

This two-hour course is taken after the learner has qualified by passing the Practical Driving Test. It seeks out the places where the new driver will face

Night Driving

If a learner does their drive during the daytime — which is when most people learn — particularly in the summer months, it is quite possible that they will gain no experience of driving in the dark. On the night-driving course, the BSM instructor will show the learner how best to cope with driving in night-time conditions.

BSM Insurance Services

> Newly-qualified and young drivers are an insurance risk...

For most new, and especially young drivers, finding affordable car insurance is time-consuming and frustrating, not to mention confusing. You will find that many insurance companies will simply not insure new drivers or drivers under certain ages.

Newly-qualified drivers are a prime target for high insurance premiums, and in addition they will not be entitled to a No Claims Discount (that is, the discount received on the renewal of their annual premium provided that the driver has made no claims on their insurance).

These two factors will typically make their insurance costs much higher than those of more experienced drivers. Moreover, insuring their car can be a complete nightmare, particularly when they are bombarded with technical jargon and loads of small print.

BSM Insurance Services has taken the stress and difficulties out of finding great-value insurance deals for all drivers by simply calling us on 08452 76 76 76.

How can you save money on your insurance premiums?

BSM strongly recommend that learners take a Pass Plus Course (see pages 153–154) with

● *There's no need to sell your grandmother to afford car insurance.*

one of our specially registered instructors, on passing their Practical Driving Test. Not only will this make them a safer driver but by completing the course they will be entitled to substantial discounts on their insurance premium, sometimes as much as 30%, the equivalent of a one year No Claim Discount.

BSM Insurance Services provides:

- A team of specially-trained sales people to assist in finding the best value-for-money deal available to BSM for the driver's benefit
- A panel of the UK's top insurance companies offering the highest quality service to BSM customers
- Uninsured loss and legal protection (ask about this if you are unsure what it means).

Please ask about other benefits which may change and be revised from time to time.

Please do:

- When the learner enquires about insurance, even if they have not completed the Pass Plus course, they should see how much more can be saved if the course is taken.

Please don't:

- The owner or main driver of a car must be insured in their own name. Insuring it in, say, a relative's name in an attempt to attract cheaper insurance may, and probably will, invalidate any claim made on the insurance in the future. It is also beneficial for the insurer to be establishing their own No Claims Bonus, which will make insurance cheaper in the future.

At BSM Insurance Services we are here to help and assist drivers beyond the passing of the Practical Driving Test, and we hope that all our learners will in the future continue to insure with us.

Free RAC Roadside Membership

Worth £44 for BSM test passers

Don't forget that BSM test passers can claim free RAC Roadside membership for a year (subject to RAC terms and conditions, available at your nearest BSM Centre).

Even if the learner does not have their own car, RAC membership is still really useful, since it covers the person and not their vehicle. Imagine the peace of mind they'll have when out with friends and family knowing that they have RAC cover should a breakdown occur.

What RAC Roadside offers

If the learner should suffer a breakdown, the RAC will fix their car at the roadside or, if that proves difficult, give them a free tow to a local garage (within 10 miles). This includes help if the car gets a flat battery, a punctured tyre or even if the learner locks themself out of their car.

Practice Sessions

A guide to accompanying the learner driver

Part
5

Practice Sessions Records

Private Practice Record

On the following pages, you will find a block for each of the 32 BSM Recommended Practice Sessions, with a note of the pages in the book where the Session appears. There are up to 4 records per session for you to fill in, but if you require more, use the blank blocks from pages 167–169.

Circle the number of the practice for each session, enter the date of the practice and circle any of the Advanced Exercises practised during the session. Finally, make a note of the time spent on each practice session.

We have filled in an example block below for you to use as a guide.

Session 1	Moving Off and Stopping on a Level Surface		pages 48–50
Practice No.	Date	Advanced Exercises	Time Spent Practising
(1)	12/ 11/00	a b (c) d	One and a half hours
(2)	3/ 1 /01	(a) b c d	2 hours, 45 minutes
3	/ /	a b c d	
4	/ /	a b c d	

Session 1	Moving Off and Stopping on a Level Surface		pages 48–50
Practice No.	Date	Advanced Exercises	Time Spent Practising
1	/ /	a b c d	
2	/ /	a b c d	
3	/ /	a b c d	
4	/ /	a b c d	

Session 2	Using the Steering Wheel		pages 51–53
Practice No.	Date	Advanced Exercises	Time Spent Practising
1	/ /	a	
2	/ /	a	
3	/ /	a	
4	/ /	a	

Session 3	Clutch Control		pages 54–55
Practice No.	Date	Advanced Practice	Time Spent Practising
1	/ /	a b c d	
2	/ /	a b c d	
3	/ /	a b c d	
4	/ /	a b c d	

Session 4	Moving Off and Stopping Uphill		pages 56–58
Practice No.	Date	Advanced Practice	Time Spent Practising
1	/ /	a b c d e	
2	/ /	a b c d e	
3	/ /	a b c d e	
4	/ /	a b c d e	

Session 5	Moving Off and Stopping Downhill		pages 59–61
Practice No.	Date	Advanced Practice	Time Spent Practising
1	/ /	a b c d	
2	/ /	a b c d	
3	/ /	a b c d	
4	/ /	a b c d	

Session 6	Changing Up to Second and Third Gear		pages 62–64
Practice No.	Date	Advanced Practice	Time Spent Practising
1	/ /	a b c d	
2	/ /	a b c d	
3	/ /	a b c d	
4	/ /	a b c d	

Session 7	Turning Left From a Major to a Minor Road		pages 65–67
Practice No.	Date	Advanced Practice	Time Spent Practising
1	/ /	a b c d e	
2	/ /	a b c d e	
3	/ /	a b c d e	
4	/ /	a b c d e	

Session 8	Emerging Left From a Minor to a Major Road		pages 68–70
Practice No.	Date	Advanced Practice	Time Spent Practising
1	/ /	a b c d e f g	
2	/ /	a b c d e f g	
3	/ /	a b c d e f g	
4	/ /	a b c d e f g	

Session 9	Turning Right From a Major to a Minor Road		pages 71–73
Practice No.	Date	Advanced Practice	Time Spent Practising
1	/ /	a b c d e f	
2	/ /	a b c d e f	
3	/ /	a b c d e f	
4	/ /	a b c d e f	

Session 10	Emerging Right From a Minor to a Major Road		pages 74–76
Practice No.	Date	Advanced Practice	Time Spent Practising
1	/ /	a b c d e f g	
2	/ /	a b c d e f g	
3	/ /	a b c d e f g	
4	/ /	a b c d e f g	

Session 11	Changing Up and Down Through All the Gears		pages 77–79
Practice No.	Date	Advanced Practice	Time Spent Practising
1	/ /	a b c d e f	
2	/ /	a b c d e f	
3	/ /	a b c d e f	
4	/ /	a b c d e f	

Session 12	Moving Off At an Angle		pages 80–82
Practice No.	Date	Advanced Practice	Time Spent Practising
1	/ /	a b c d	
2	/ /	a b c d	
3	/ /	a b c d	
4	/ /	a b c d	

Session 13	Reversing Around a Corner to the Left		pages 83–85
Practice No.	Date	Advanced Practice	Time Spent Practising
1	/ /	a b c d e	
2	/ /	a b c d e	
3	/ /	a b c d e	
4	/ /	a b c d e	

Session 14	Reversing Around a Corner to the Right		pages 86–88
Practice No.	Date	Advanced Practice	Time Spent Practising
1	/ /	a b c d e	
2	/ /	a b c d e	
3	/ /	a b c d e	
4	/ /	a b c d e	

Session 15	Turning the Car in the Road		pages 89–91
Practice No.	Date	Advanced Practice	Time Spent Practising
1	/ /	a b c d e	
2	/ /	a b c d e	
3	/ /	a b c d e	
4	/ /	a b c d e	

Session 16	Reversing into a Parking Space		pages 92–94
Practice No.	Date	Advanced Practice	Time Spent Practising
1	/ /	a b c d e	
2	/ /	a b c d e	
3	/ /	a b c d e	
4	/ /	a b c d e	

Session 17	Reverse Parking		pages 95–97
Practice No.	Date	Advanced Practice	Time Spent Practising
1	/ /	a b c d e	
2	/ /	a b c d e	
3	/ /	a b c d e	
4	/ /	a b c d e	

Session 18	Using Mirrors Effectively		pages 98–99
Practice No.	Date	Advanced Practice	Time Spent Practising
1	/ /	a b c d	
2	/ /	a b c d	
3	/ /	a b c d	
4	/ /	a b c d	

Session 19	Giving Signals		pages 100–102
Practice No.	Date	Advanced Practice	Time Spent Practising
1	/ /	a b c	
2	/ /	a b c	
3	/ /	a b c	
4	/ /	a b c	

Session 20	Dealing With Crossroads		pages 103–105
Practice No.	Date	Advanced Practice	Time Spent Practising
1	/ /	a b c d e	
2	/ /	a b c d e	
3	/ /	a b c d e	
4	/ /	a b c d e	

Session 21	Dealing With Roundabouts		pages 106–108
Practice No.	Date	Advanced Practice	Time Spent Practising
1	/ /	a b c d e f	
2	/ /	a b c d e f	
3	/ /	a b c d e f	
4	/ /	a b c d e f	

Session 22	Dealing With Pedestrian Crossings		pages 109–111
Practice No.	Date	Advanced Practice	Time Spent Practising
1	/ /	a b c d e	
2	/ /	a b c d e	
3	/ /	a b c d e	
4	/ /	a b c d e	

Session 23	Road Position and Lane Discipline		pages 112–114
Practice No.	Date	Advanced Practice	Time Spent Practising
1	/ /	a b	
2	/ /	a b	
3	/ /	a b	
4	/ /	a b	

Session 24	Care in the Use of Speed		pages 115–117
Practice No.	Date	Advanced Practice	Time Spent Practising
1	/ /	a b c d	
2	/ /	a b c d	
3	/ /	a b c d	
4	/ /	a b c d	

Session 25	Keeping Space from Traffic		pages 118–120
Practice No.	Date	Advanced Practice	Time Spent Practising
1	/ /	a b c d	
2	/ /	a b c d	
3	/ /	a b c d	
4	/ /	a b c d	

Session 26	Meeting Other Traffic		pages 121–123
Practice No.	Date	Advanced Practice	Time Spent Practising
1	/ /	a b c d	
2	/ /	a b c d	
3	/ /	a b c d	
4	/ /	a b c d	

Session 27	Dealing With Dual Carriageways		pages 124–126
Practice No.	Date	Advanced Practice	Time Spent Practising
1	/ /	a b c d	
2	/ /	a b c d	
3	/ /	a b c d	
4	/ /	a b c d	

Session 28	Overtaking		pages 127–129
Practice No.	Date	Advanced Practice	Time Spent Practising
1	/ /	a b c d e f	
2	/ /	a b c d e f	
3	/ /	a b c d e f	
4	/ /	a b c d e f	

Session 29	Assessing Risks		pages 130–132
Practice No.	Date	Advanced Practice	Time Spent Practising
1	/ /	a b c d	
2	/ /	a b c d	
3	/ /	a b c d	
4	/ /	a b c d	

Session 30	Commentary Driving		pages 133–135
Practice No.	Date	Advanced Practice	Time Spent Practising
1	/ /	a b c d	
2	/ /	a b c d	
3	/ /	a b c d	
4	/ /	a b c d	

Session 31	Night Driving		pages 136–138
Practice No.	Date	Advanced Practice	Time Spent Practising
1	/ /	a b c d e f g	
2	/ /	a b c d e f g	
3	/ /	a b c d e f g	
4	/ /	a b c d e f g	

Session 32	Driving in Bad Weather		pages 139–141
Practice No.	Date	Advanced Practice	Time Spent Practising
1	/ /	a b c	
2	/ /	a b c	
3	/ /	a b c	
4	/ /	a b c	

Session No:____ Subject:_____			
Practice No.	Date	Advanced Practice	Time Spent Practising
1	/ /	a b c d e f g	
2	/ /	a b c d e f g	
3	/ /	a b c d e f g	
4	/ /	a b c d e f g	

Session No:____ Subject:_____			
Practice No.	Date	Advanced Practice	Time Spent Practising
1	/ /	a b c d e f g	
2	/ /	a b c d e f g	
3	/ /	a b c d e f g	
4	/ /	a b c d e f g	

Session No:____ Subject:_____			
Practice No.	Date	Advanced Practice	Time Spent Practising
1	/ /	a b c d e f g	
2	/ /	a b c d e f g	
3	/ /	a b c d e f g	
4	/ /	a b c d e f g	

Session No:____ Subject:_____			
Practice No.	Date	Advanced Practice	Time Spent Practising
1	/ /	a b c d e f g	
2	/ /	a b c d e f g	
3	/ /	a b c d e f g	
4	/ /	a b c d e f g	

Session No:____ Subject:_____			
Practice No.	Date	Advanced Practice	Time Spent Practising
1	/ /	a b c d e f g	
2	/ /	a b c d e f g	
3	/ /	a b c d e f g	
4	/ /	a b c d e f g	

Session No: _____ Subject: _____			
Practice No.	Date	Advanced Practice	Time Spent Practising
1	/ /	a b c d e f g	
2	/ /	a b c d e f g	
3	/ /	a b c d e f g	
4	/ /	a b c d e f g	

Session No: _____ Subject: _____			
Practice No.	Date	Advanced Practice	Time Spent Practising
1	/ /	a b c d e f g	
2	/ /	a b c d e f g	
3	/ /	a b c d e f g	
4	/ /	a b c d e f g	

Session No: _____ Subject: _____			
Practice No.	Date	Advanced Practice	Time Spent Practising
1	/ /	a b c d e f g	
2	/ /	a b c d e f g	
3	/ /	a b c d e f g	
4	/ /	a b c d e f g	

Session No: _____ Subject: _____			
Practice No.	Date	Advanced Practice	Time Spent Practising
1	/ /	a b c d e f g	
2	/ /	a b c d e f g	
3	/ /	a b c d e f g	
4	/ /	a b c d e f g	

Session No: _____ Subject: _____			
Practice No.	Date	Advanced Practice	Time Spent Practising
1	/ /	a b c d e f g	
2	/ /	a b c d e f g	
3	/ /	a b c d e f g	
4	/ /	a b c d e f g	

Session No:	Subject:		
Practice No.	Date	Advanced Practice	Time Spent Practising
1	/ /	a b c d e f g	
2	/ /	a b c d e f g	
3	/ /	a b c d e f g	
4	/ /	a b c d e f g	

Session No:	Subject:		
Practice No.	Date	Advanced Practice	Time Spent Practising
1	/ /	a b c d e f g	
2	/ /	a b c d e f g	
3	/ /	a b c d e f g	
4	/ /	a b c d e f g	

Session No:	Subject:		
Practice No.	Date	Advanced Practice	Time Spent Practising
1	/ /	a b c d e f g	
2	/ /	a b c d e f g	
3	/ /	a b c d e f g	
4	/ /	a b c d e f g	

Session No:	Subject:		
Practice No.	Date	Advanced Practice	Time Spent Practising
1	/ /	a b c d e f g	
2	/ /	a b c d e f g	
3	/ /	a b c d e f g	
4	/ /	a b c d e f g	

Session No:	Subject:		
Practice No.	Date	Advanced Practice	Time Spent Practising
1	/ /	a b c d e f g	
2	/ /	a b c d e f g	
3	/ /	a b c d e f g	
4	/ /	a b c d e f g	

Notes & Comments

The four following pages are for the BSM instructor and the learner's accompanying driver to record any specific information relating to the Practice Sessions which might be useful in determining further practice.

Date	BSM Instructor's Comments	Accompanying Driver's Comments

Notes & Comments

Date	BSM Instructor's Comments	Accompanying Driver's Comments

Notes & Comments

Date	BSM Instructor's Comments	Accompanying Driver's Comments

Notes & Comments

Date	BSM Instructor's Comments	Accompanying Driver's Comments

BSM Instructor Recommendations

The columns below show the date of the lesson with the BSM instructor, together with the Practice Session and Advanced Exercises the learner has been recommended to undertake with their accompanying driver before attending their next BSM lesson.

Date	Practice Session Recommended	Advanced Exercise(s) Recommended

Date	Practice Session Recommended	Advanced Exercise(s) Recommended

Date	Practice Session Recommended	Advanced Exercise(s) Recommended